ADVANCE PRAISE FOR
CRISIS OF COMMAND

"Unpopular views are always hard to hear until they prove to be true. What Stuart Scheller has to say is critical for the military and nation."

–LtCol Oliver North, USMC. Vietnam Veteran. Silver Star. Bronze Stars. Purple Hearts.

"Those of us who wear the uniform took an oath: to support and defend the Constitution of the United States. The President and all Members of Congress took that same oath. It is a commitment to put the interests of our country first. Those who are not committed to this cause should not hold positions of power in our government. LtCol Stu Scheller's unique perspective will spark conversations and questions about leadership and accountability that are necessary to bring about positive change."

–Tulsi Gabbard, United States Army Reserves, Former Congresswoman, Former Presidential Candidate. Iraq War Veteran. Combat Medical Badge.

"If your reaction to the botched American withdrawal from Afghanistan was, 'what the f@#%,' this book is a MUST read. Marine Lt-Col Scheller, jailed for demanding accountability, offers hard truths to the Pentagon's top brass. If the military wants to prevent the next failure, they should start listening to leaders like LtCol Scheller."

–Congressman Brian Mast, United States Army. Afghan Veteran. Bronze Star. Purple Heart.

"*Crisis of Command* is raw, real, and courageous, just like Stuart Scheller. Stuart is a man on a mission, and the country needs him now more than ever. He is an intelligent, educated, combat tested, and command selected superior warfighter. Now he's calling out our so-called 'leaders' who have failed the mission, troops, and nation."

–Pete Hegseth, Army National Guard, Fox and Friends Host. Afghan Veteran. Bronze Stars.

"We are in a crisis of leadership at the senior levels in the military. Senior military leaders have failed over the last two decades. The book *Crisis of Command* addresses the shortfalls perfectly. We need more people like Stuart Scheller with the courage to challenge the system. The future of America depends upon it."

-General Don Bolduc, United States Army. Ten tours in Afghanistan. Bronze Stars. Purple Hearts.

CRISIS

— OF —

COMMAND

HOW WE LOST
TRUST AND CONFIDENCE
IN AMERICA'S
GENERALS AND POLITICIANS

STUART SCHELLER

FORMER LT. COL. USMC

A KNOX PRESS BOOK
An Imprint of Permuted Press
ISBN: 978-1-63758-544-3
ISBN (eBook): 978-1-63758-545-0

Crisis of Command:
How We Lost Trust and Confidence in America's Generals and
Politicians
© 2022 by Stuart Scheller
All Rights Reserved

Cover Art by Cody Corcoran
Interior Design by Yoni Limor

Permuted Press, LLC
New York • Nashville
permutedpress.com

Published in the United States of America
1 2 3 4 5 6 7 8 9 10

I'd like to dedicate this book to the following three groups:

My three sons. I hope this book one day helps you understand the circumstances surrounding my decisions. I love you three more than anything. I will spend the rest of my life demonstrating the behavior required of an American man and father.

My parents. I distanced myself from you for the seventeen years I served in the Marine Corps. But like true warriors, you showed up when the fight began, and defended me in my time of need. I appreciate your love and support. I will spend the rest of my life proving I was worth the sacrifices.

The American people. You supported me in my time of need. I truly believe the American people are the most compassionate people in the world. I will spend the rest of my life dedicated to making this nation better for all of US.

TABLE OF CONTENTS

PREFACE

My name is Stuart Scheller. I am the seventeen-year Marine Corps infantry officer who resigned at the rank of lieutenant colonel after witnessing a poorly planned and executed Afghanistan withdraw. I was thrust into the media when I posted a video on Facebook and LinkedIn from my office as a battalion commander. Wearing my uniform, I identified myself in the video with rank and title and then proceeded to criticize the decisions of my senior military and political leaders. A series of escalating events occurred following the release of the video, which resulted in my imprisonment, court-martial, and resignation.

The central question I had for my senior leaders then, and still have today: How can the greatest military power in the world tolerate keeping those in power who continually squander the lives and treasure of the American people? I have unpopular theories to the question. I wrote this book because senior military leaders and politicians demonstrate an inability to engage or acknowledge obvious failures. I dedicated my life to this country. I led service members into battle who died fighting for the initiatives of our senior leaders. We win all the tactical battles, yet when it is time to link our tactical success to operational and strategic goals, the United States consistently fails.

This is my story. This is my perspective. Why I joined the Marine Corps. Why I love America. Why I joined during a time of war, and why I wanted combat experiences. How I progressed through my career. How my experiences in places like Iraq and Afghanistan shaped my thinking. How my military education created deeper questions about America's foreign policy approach. And how the events of Afghanistan compelled me to sacrifice everything in my life up to that point.

The book is structured as follows: Chapter 1 jumps straight to the suicide attack at Kabul, Afghanistan, airfield on August 26, 2021. Chapter 2 starts with my enlistment into the Marine Corps in 2004, and the story progresses in a linear fashion thereafter. Chapters 2 through 9 describe my career prior to the Afghanistan withdrawal. This section is relevant for the reader's understanding of my perspective and experiences and overlays my career within a time frame that America conducted two of its longest wars. It's a glimpse into my generation's struggles during those wars. Additionally, my personal and family life permeates each chapter of the story. This additional storyline illustrates an often-untold baseline for the pressure applied to families impacted by a military career.

Chapters 10 through 17 describe the struggle I endured with the Marine Corps after I posted my first video. There are many hard truths in this portion of the book, but transparency is critical for evolution. I hope service members learn something about addressing failures of the bureaucracy. More than that, I hope all Americans open their eyes to the fundamental problems facing the military. The executive branch, legislative branch, and military system have demonstrated unwillingness to make the changes required. If American citizens can't force reform on the military, the United States' ability to enhance power in the foreign policy arena will continue degrading. America's evolution requires acknowledging failure and breakdowns in the system apolitically. My son's future depends upon it.

INTRODUCTION

"The great political conflict of our century, I believe, is that between a networked public and the elites who inhabit the great hierarchical institutions that organize modern life... The public, which swims comfortably in the digital sea, knows far more than elites trapped in obsolete structures. The public knows when the elites fail to deliver their promised 'solutions,' when they tell falsehoods or misspeak, when they are caught in sexual escapades, and when they indulge in astonishing levels of smugness and hypocrisy. The public is disenchanted in the elites and their institutions... To maintain the authority of institutions, an explanation must be provided to the public that connects events to the ideal. The moments of defeat are always instructive."

—Antonio Martinez in The Prophet of the Revolt

The United States military's obligation is winning wars. Period. Since World War II, the United States military has continued losing wars. Period. Military generals have insulated themselves from accountability of failed wars by deflecting blame toward politicians and adjacent foreign diplomacy departments. This excuse cannot be tolerated much longer without great risk to the American people. Addressing the American military's problems through action will increase chances of success in a future war. Unfortunately, there is no simple solution to the military's problems. Military planners would refer to it as a wicked problem. I will call it a complex problem. And solving complex problems requires pulling on one thread at a time.

The problem affecting all other shortfalls originates from how generals obtain their positions. Promotion only occurs in the military when service members receive favorable evaluations from their superiors. Military members receive favorable evaluations by reflecting the ideas and beliefs of their superiors. As service members climb the career ladder, at each step of promotion, they become susceptible to veering away from a warfighting focus. Reflecting the status quo ideology of a boss is the easiest way to promotion. Currently, warfighting capability and winning wars are not priorities for promotion. A warfighting focus may factor into the boss's impression of a military employee, but it is a small slice at most. I witnessed several talented officers wash out of the system because their warfighting focus detracted from the peripheral tasks prioritized by superiors.

The military system heavily favors those who focus on career progression. Focusing on career progression at times develops an officer's warfighting skills, but at other times it detracts from it. In the current military bureaucracy, promotion is not synonymous with the necessary ideals of militaristic command. Ultimately, we have people in critical leadership positions making egregious errors because they simply are not prepared for the job. Despite the systemic failures, senior military leaders must be held accountable.

To be clear, accountability doesn't solve the problem. Fixing the promotion system, career path ladder, and culture of the military should be the long-term approach. However, accountability does cause a course correction. When Americans begin holding senior military leaders accountable, it forces acknowledgment from military leaders that in addition to pleasing their bosses they must also focus on winning wars.

The military hierarchal institution, built by the greatness of each military branch's forefathers, is rarely questioned in terms of foundational effectiveness. Instead, the path to mediocrity is continually refined within these systems. The military officer career progression is one such pathway. Leaders now require subordinates to move through small choke points of career advancement. The "career roadmap" is yet another mechanism for conformism. Modern military leaders degrade fresh perspectives by moving service members through narrow paths designed to imitate predecessors' experiences. While the system should replicate the experiences of senior leaders, if senior leaders consistently fail in their primary task of winning wars, then the path should obviously be reexamined. Additionally, choke points deemed essential to the organization, but absent any correlation to warfighting, have been inappropriately prioritized for promotion. When or if changes do occur in thinking or approach, they are incremental at best. The military in large part, due to a lack of fresh perspective and critical thinking, demonstrates an inability to fundamentally change at the pace required to maintain competitive advantage.

Senior generals are promoted based on their willingness to please superiors. Said another way, they are promoted because they don't push back. Thus, when General Kenneth F. McKenzie addressed why he withdrew military forces in Afghanistan during the peak fighting season before evacuating American citizens, his justification, "I was following the orders I was given," was not surprising. Sadly, it's also not surprising that General Carter Ham, when ordered, stood down military response forces during the Benghazi incident. His blind obedience to orders resulted in Americans dying needlessly. There is predictability in both responses when people understand General McKenzie and General Ham became senior military leaders by not pushing back on authority. Unfortunately for Americans, courageous people are needed now more than ever in the senior military ranks. As a product of our promotion system, senior military leaders wholistically don't have the ability to disobey orders in commonsense moments.

As you may have heard in the media, the military depicted me as the bad guy.

Yes, I did break the rules.

Yes, I should have been held accountable.

And so should every senior leader for their violations. However, they only acknowledge the failures of those below them and lack the courage, fortitude, and wherewithal to acknowledge the failures of their counterparts at the top. My story is a microcosm for the hypocrisy of the system.

The culture of "yes men" at the senior military ranks is not an easy fix. In any other industry, companies bring in new ideas and approaches by hiring professionals from other firms. The practice of cross-pollination does not exist in the military. The military promotion system is strictly time based. A commander in chief has limited military reform options within the current system. Short of legislating reform for the outdated Goldwater-Nichols system, the president is relegated to appointing a secretary of defense who understands the problems and has the courage to dramatically reshuffle senior officers.

This closed military system is further destabilized by a culture of nepotism. A large portion of battalion commanders right now are sons of other generals. Children of generals are not given a free pass. And many of them are very talented. But when people have small advantages, these advantages build up over time. These systemic advantages exist and need to be acknowledged. Malcolm Gladwell in his book *Outliers* developed an example through data illustrating the parallel. Gladwell noticed that the birth months for professional hockey players overwhelmingly fell in the first months of a given year. Their birthdate provided a small size and maturity advantage. This small advantage allowed them to make all the competitive teams at a young age, which allowed them to develop at a faster pace. This development provided more opportunities to become professional players. A similar pattern occurs in the highest levels of the military. The sons of generals already have a successful battle plan mapped out for them. They are cognizant of the actions needed to make their careers more marketable for promotion. Through namesakes and a knowledge of how to play the system, they build and exploit nonlinear advantages over others. This is relevant if the military struggles with producing a new type of senior military leader with courage and fresh perspective. Not only are the heirs less likely to take risks and think differently, but their entrance into the military also immediately impacts their fathers' thinking; senior generals with sons in the military are more likely to play it safe for their namesakes.

The gender and racial equality topics of the last decade are also addressed in this book. There was no avoiding the conversation if you served in the military for the last two decades. To clarify up front, equality and equal opportunity are two very different things, yet the distinction between these separate issues is often conflated within the military. Every American wants their sons and daughters to have an opportunity to serve in the military under one equal standard. Not every American wants their sons and daughters treated differently based on race or gender for the appearance of diversity.

In addition to the diversity priorities, senior military leaders have also increasingly placed an emphasis on a perception of ethics. On the surface, no one would disagree with the utility of ethics. Americans pride themselves on ethics, morals, and an idealistic outlook. However, these attributes are only meaningful in war when transformed into lethal power. At times these attributes can detract from, rather than enhance, America's ability to win wars. I believe in God. I believe in good and evil. But I also believe American service members are sacrificing unnecessarily for the system's perception of ethics. Americans need more realism injected into their foreign policy decisions. The "just war theory" is wrong. There are no "just" wars. Only wars. The "just" portion is all about spinning a narrative. I acknowledge the military is more lethal when humans fighting for a nation-state believe they are on the "just" side of the war. However, America now wages war over long timelines, debilitated by unnecessary restrictions, all without clear objectives or political end states in the name of "justice." The system is failing the junior service member.

Moreover, the contracting, procurement, and spending processes are widely recognized in the defense industry for their inefficiencies and failed practices. There exists an oligopoly within the government contracting world reaping exorbitant amounts of money off the war industry. This small group of firms hires people like James Mattis and Lloyd Austin and places them like puppets on boards of directors, where they earn hundreds of thousands of dollars annually to garner influence with the general officer community. Meanwhile, a young, enlisted infantryman cannot receive basic technology in a timely manner due to bureaucratic red tape in procurement. Instead, the junior service member consistently and unknowingly assumes unnecessary risks because the procurement process cannot be navigated effectively by senior military leaders. The commonly used Marine Corps' Amphibious Assault Vehicle, extended decades beyond its service life, still exists because of the problems with procurement. Yet despite these problems, the Department of Defense budget continues growing while military leaders incentivize spending taxpayer dollars as quickly as possible.

Finally, the military has tolerated a toxic leadership culture in the senior ranks for far too long. A senior leader's opportunity during command is critical for promotion regardless of the job's operational significance. There are many talented and compassionate commanders in the military. But far too often toxic leaders are promoted by squeezing every ounce of performance out of their men. Every commander gets one shot. A commander's one shot is their most important opportunity for promotion regardless of operational significance. Commanders have figured out that the quickest way to success is ensuring key members in the command work disproportionate hours at great personal costs. Obviously, over a long-enough timeline, this is not sustainable for those high performers without sacrifice. Furthermore, contempt, often heightened by a lack of sleep, develops in high performers and inevitably becomes directed toward others not working the same schedules. These individuals naturally become confrontational and entitled. And often not recognized, but important to illustrate, these attributes become more pronounced the longer a service member remains in the system. It's a systemic failure not a personality failure. Thus, any attempt to focus on these problems at the junior ranks is misguided. The commandant of the Marine Corps, General David H. Berger, acknowledged the symptom but misdiagnosed the problem. Addressing the findings of his internal 360 Review, the commandant stated to reporters, "We have to treat people like human beings instead of inventory." However, General Berger, like all commandants of the past, focuses on the O-5 (lieutenant colonel) commander level and below. The leaders at the O-6 (colonel) and above level set the tone and have more influence than all others. They are pressurizing the field-grade officers and developing the symptoms identified at the junior ranks. The secretary of defense needs to identify toxic leadership at the O-6 and above levels in all services and remove them immediately.

The internal problems of the military should be a grave concern for the general public. National power correlates to military power. The acronym DIME stands for Diplomacy, Information, Military, and Economic. These four basic tenants are a model for how a country can evaluate sources of national power. There are other complicated models, but the simple DIME model illustrates the point. The aggregate sum of America's national power, or DIME, in relation to other nations, determines America's influence on the global order. While military leaders' primary concern is winning wars, they must also possess a broader understanding of the interconnectedness of DIME so they can best advise political leadership on strategy. America's foreign policy strategy should increase national power at a pace above or commensurate with competitors, while not recklessly engaging in power draining engagements.

War materializes when a nation's diplomacy, economic, and information sources of power are not capable of influencing an enemy to the degree that political ambitions require. The military source of power is the instrument used to win wars. When politicians set war objectives, military senior leaders should be held responsible for accomplishing those objectives. The military's purpose can never be isolated from political objectives. Winning wars requires compelling an enemy's acceptance of political objectives through violence. If the United States continues allowing ineptitude at the senior military leadership level, not only will the objectives of the war fail, but all other sources of power will degrade at accelerated rates. The military source of power affects all things. In an era of global competition, Americans must improve the strength of the military immediately. This starts by addressing the failures of the senior military leaders.

The time is now for Americans to demand accountability from their senior military leadership. Americans control congressional representatives. Congressional representatives control the Defense Department budget. The military can't function without money. Americans can instantly force change in the military by demanding their representatives hold the military accountable through the budget.

If you don't believe how bad it is, please read the rest of the story.

CHAPTER 1:

SOMEBODY NEEDED TO SAY IT— AFGHANISTAN FAILURE. THIRTEEN SERVICE MEMBERS. FIRST VIDEO.

"His Majesty made you a Major because he believed you would know when not to obey his orders."

—Prince Frederick Charles

I commanded my first Marine Corps battalion the months of July and August 2021 as I watched the events of Afghanistan unfold in real time. It was painful to watch. The American military withdrew troops before evacuating American citizens. Perhaps American leaders didn't expect the Afghanistan government to fall so quickly, but their inability to build a plan based on rational thought, contingencies, or foresight was almost unbelievable. Their list of mistakes was inexcusable. They conducted the withdrawal during the peak fighting season. I knew from my time in Afghanistan that the Taliban hid in the mountains of Pakistan during the winter. In the spring they came out of the mountains, and the fighting ensued. The Americans could have exercised tactical patience and conducted the withdrawal from November to February unmolested by the Taliban. Instead, they conducted it from April to September, the most contested time of year. Then the military planners did the unthinkable: they evacuated the critical piece of infrastructure required for a successful evacuation, Bagram Air Base. It was nauseating trying to comprehend the logic while reflecting on all our sacrifices in the country.

General McKenzie, a United States Marine and the theater combatant commander at the time, went on to explain that President Biden ordered a drawdown of American military forces in Afghanistan from April to July of 2021. The order specifically stipulated a drop from 2,500 to 650 military personnel. General McKenzie may not have agreed with the president's order, but as he would later state, "he was following the orders he was given." When the president gave the order in April 2021, General McKenzie began withdrawing military troops. Concurrently he assigned General Farrell J. Sullivan, a one-star Marine general, to plan a follow-on evacuation. General Sullivan, solely focused on the evacuation, planned on Bagram Air Base as the staging point for the evacuation. But unexpectedly in the end of June 2021, General McKenzie, late in the planning process, decided to abandon Bagram Air Base. He later justified the decision by stating 650 troops was not a large enough military force to hold the embassy, Kabul airfield, and Bagram Air Base. He never addressed why three months of planning were lost because of his indecisiveness. His inability to articulate his intent based on the president's restraints forced General Sullivan to rewrite the evacuation plans only two months before the event took place. General McKenzie, solely focused on his military responsibilities and not his responsibilities to the American people, later asserted the military wasn't responsible for the failed evacuation because it was a Department of State function. This was disingenuous at best. General Sullivan and his planners began interagency planning with the Department of State in April 2021. The evacuation didn't occur until the end of August

2021. Clearly all the planners and commanders had a responsibility to figure out a wholistic approach to the evacuation.

Congressional testimony later between Representative Seth Moulton, a Democrat from Massachusetts, and General McKenzie best summarized the problem.

> "General McKenzie, you went from 2,500 troops in Afghanistan in April to 650 in July. And then turned around and put 5,000 back into Kabul. You've said repeatedly that you personally believed the Afghan government would fall if we didn't maintain a certain number of troops in country. So why didn't you plan for an evacuation and leave enough troops on the ground to conduct it."

> "So, let's be very clear. The evacuation has to be ordered by the Department of State. The drawdown of forces was ordered by the President in April and completed in July. The non-combatant evacuation operation is a separate mission. And it wasn't completely under the control of the Department of Defense."

> "So, you're going to fall back on the bureaucracy. The divide between the Department of Defense and State? That's the reason you had to pull back all those troops and then had to put more back in?"

> "I'm going to fall back on the orders I was given, Representative."

I continued monitoring the situation in August 2021 as the Taliban swept through Afghanistan in a matter of weeks. The

Taliban walked into Bagram Air base on August 10 unopposed. At the base they found thousands of weapons, vehicles, and most importantly five to seven thousand prisoners left by the Americans in the prison. The discovery instantly swelled the Taliban's force. Most likely the suicide bomber who later attacked the Marines originated from the prison.

I watched multiple units, including my first unit, First Battalion, Eighth Marines, rapidly respond to a situation poorly planned for months. I knew from experience junior service members on the ground would rise to the occasion despite failures at the general officer level, but I remained frustrated at the situation.

General Berger, the commandant of the Marine Corps, on August 18 released a message to the force addressing the deteriorating situation on the ground and the negative reaction across the force. In the letter General Berger stated:

> As each of us tries to comprehend the speed and scope of events in Afghanistan this week, some may be struggling with a simple question: "Was it all worth it?"... We [Sergeant Major Black and I] believe—without question—that your service was meaningful, powerful, and important.... You fought to prevent terror from returning to our shores.... Whether you realize it or not, you set an example for subsequent generations of Marines—and Americans—by living our core values of Honor, Courage, and Commitment. Was it worth it? Yes.

I felt a deep rage burning in my belly after reading the letter. If the commandant had any Honor, Courage, and Commitment, he would have acknowledged why service members were so frustrated. They were frustrated by the way the withdrawal/evacuation was conducted. They were frustrated that senior leaders let them down.

The commandant either didn't understand or didn't care. Either way, he wasn't advocating for his Marines.

The very same day, the Pentagon released a statement addressing the same frustrations across the military service. The Pentagon also failed addressing any failures at the senior leader level but instead victimized the service members by projecting mental health problems as a source of the frustration. The Pentagon statement said:

> Talking can be very therapeutic, whether it's to a local chaplain, psychologist or someone you served with in the military. Do what feels right for you. There is not one way to think or feel or act. The important thing is to take advantage of the numerous mental health care resources that are available to you. Remember that this is one moment in time and regardless of what comes next, we will get through it together.

That weekend I was so overtly upset my wife asked me what was bothering me. At the time I sat in front of our fish tank. We had four turtles and a collection of fish. Watching the aquarium creatures eased my anxiety. "It's hard to put into words how frustrated I am about this Afghanistan withdrawal," I told her. "I've spent my whole life dedicated to a cause that now appears hollow. The words Honor, Courage, Commitment are a bumper sticker."

My wife didn't know what to say. She listened, and then walked back into the kitchen with the kids while I continued staring at the fish. The following Thursday, August 26, I found myself sitting in my office when the suicide vest attack occurred in Afghanistan.

The news of the attack first came across the open source media. My battalion executive officer walked into my office to speak with me about it.

"Did you hear about the attack, sir? This is bullshit. How could we fuck it up this bad?"

My executive officer's comments summarized every Marine's sentiment. How did we fuck it up that bad? Everyone was angry. Everyone was disappointed with our senior leaders. They continued to let us down. They continued placing career progression over warfighting capability. They continued redirecting blame in every direction but at themselves. They were all hypocrites. They didn't represent anything about our core ethos. But I couldn't complain to my Marines. I let my executive officer release his frustrations and then sent him on his way. That afternoon two more staff members stopped by my office to vent. I continued conveying the party line. I told them casualties were a part of war, but I knew in my soul I was being disingenuous at best. At worst, I was degrading my very core belief system by lying for our senior leaders. When I finally had a moment alone, I realized I also needed an outlet. I thought about discussing my frustrations with my regimental commander, but then I remembered that despite his thirty years of service in the infantry, he had never been to Afghanistan. I briefly thought about filing a request mast—the right of any Marine to be able to communicate grievances to a commanding officer—or inspector general complaint, but I knew those processes would be blocked by the same bureaucratic red tape that got us into the mess in the first place. I was trapped in a midlevel position, with no real authority or recourse to address our systemic failures.

Sitting at my computer I began writing out my frustrations. I wrote a two-page paper demanding accountability from my senior leaders. After writing the speech I thought about submitting it to a professional publication, but as I read over it, I realized it was way too honest for any publication. I knew most military publications were controlled by the retired generals or corporate media with their own agendas. Yet, I was convinced someone needed to say the exact words typed out on my computer. I knew my senior leaders didn't have the courage to say it. Career progression was too important to them. That's when I started thinking about making a video. I thought, *If I make a video demanding accountability from my senior leaders and post it, I will probably get fired. I'm not sure that's worth it. But if I'm going to take the risk, then it needs to have the maximum effect possible. The only way to do this is all the way. I continued to wrestle with the idea. I can make it and then decide not to post it, I rationalized.*

After struggling with the moral dilemma, while sitting in my office in uniform, I ultimately decided to make a video demanding accountability. The video can still be found all over the internet. I said the following:

> Good evening, my name is LtCol Stu Scheller United States Marine Corps. I'm the current battalion commander for Advanced Infantry Training Battalion. I've been in the Marine infantry for seventeen years. I'm making this video because I have a growing discontent and contempt for my perceived ineptitude at the foreign policy level. And I want to specifically ask some questions to some of my senior leaders. And I'll say, that as a person who is not at twenty years, I feel like I have a lot to lose. I've thought through if I post this video what might happen to me, especially if the video picks up traction. If I have the courage to post it.

At this point I pause and stare directly at the camera and state:

> But I think what you believe in can only be defined by what you are willing to risk. So if I'm willing to risk my battalion commander seat, my retirement, and my family's stability to say some of the things that I want to say, I think it gives me some moral high ground to demand the same honesty, integrity, and accountability from my senior leaders.

7

I then reference the Pentagon and commandant's deflective statements delivered to the force the previous week. I then look back at the camera and continue:

> But the reason people are so upset right now is not because the Marine on the battlefield let someone down. That service member has always rose [*sic*] to the occasion and done extraordinary things. People are upset because their senior leaders have let them down, and none of them are raising their hand and accepting accountability or saying we messed this up. If an O-5 battalion commander has the simplest live fire incident or equal opportunity complaint...boom...fired. But we have a secretary of defense who testified to Congress in May that the Afghan National Security Force could withstand the Taliban advance. We have a chairman of the joint chiefs, who the commandant is a member of, who is supposed to advise on military policy. We have a Marine combatant commander. All of these people are supposed to advise. And I'm not saying we have to be in Afghanistan forever, but I am saying, did any of you throw your rank on the table and say it's a bad idea to evacuate Bagram Air Base before we evacuated everyone? Did any of you do that? And when you didn't think to do that, did any of you raise your hand and say we completely messed this up?

I then referenced a peer of mine, Lieutenant Colonel Nash, the son of a general officer and an adjacent battalion commander, who made a post stating the same thing as all my senior leaders. Every statement I read concluded that service members' sacrifices were "worth it" despite the failures. None of them acknowledged senior leaders' failures or courageously addressed what really needed to be said. So I addressed the concern:

> Potentially all of those people did die in vain if we don't have senior leaders that own up and raise their hand and say we did not do this well in the end. Without that we just keep repeating the same mistakes. This amalgamation of the economic, corporate, political, and higher military ranks are not holding up their end of the bargain. I want to say this very strongly, I have been fighting for seventeen years, I am willing to throw it all away to say to my senior leaders, I demand accountability.

I recorded about five takes of the video from my iPhone. By the fifth take I was content with the content. But at that point I still didn't have the courage to post the video. I left work that night around 19:00 and drove back to my house. The entire thirty-minute drive I thought about my dilemma. *Should I post the video? What would happen to my family if I posted the video? Was it worth it? Should I sleep on it? Should I delete it?*

I pulled into my driveway around 19:30. I sat in the driveway for at least five minutes lost in my thoughts. While sitting in the truck, I loaded the video to Facebook but still couldn't bring myself to hit the post button. I got out of the truck and stared at the front door of my house. I couldn't enter. I paced back and forth on the sidewalk in front of my house staring at the post button. I walked back and forth probably ten times. I knew if I walked back in the house and slept on it, I wouldn't have the courage to post it the next day. This was important. This was my entire life's work. Finally I thought to myself, *If not me, then who? If not now, then when?* In that moment I was filled with a sense of purpose. I hit post.

CHAPTER 2:

I'M LOOKING FOR PURPOSE—
SOCCER. ACCOUNTING. MARINE.

"Always bear in mind that your own resolution to succeed is more important than any other one thing."

—Abraham Lincoln

I grew up in a loving and supportive household. I had two younger brothers and a younger sister. We were all within six years of each other. My father was an insurance salesman, and my mother was a stay-at-home mom. Other than school, I spent most of my youth playing sports. At one point I played on almost every type of sports team: baseball, basketball, football, hockey, swimming, soccer, track, and cross-country. Soccer became my full-time sport by the time I went to high school. I made the varsity team as a freshman. By my senior year I distinguished myself as an Ohio all-state player and was my conference player of the year. I enjoyed soccer and hanging out with friends more than school, but at the same time I recognized the importance of grades. I put in the required work and made the honor roll. I maintained between a 3.5 and 4.0 average throughout my high school career.

My father always told me I needed a college degree to be successful. Military service was not discussed as a serious option in my house. In fact, my experience with the ASVAB test (Armed Services Vocational Aptitude Battery) in high school illustrated my apathetic attitude toward military service. Instead of taking the test seriously, I challenged the guy next to me to see how fast we could fill in the bubbles of the scantron. It didn't seem worth my time. I was convinced military service wasn't in my future. College was the path charted for me by my family. At that time, I didn't have much appreciation for the world outside my circle of influence.

After the soccer season ended my senior year of high school, I accepted a full-ride scholarship playing soccer at Cumberland College (now known as the University of Cumberland). It was a small Baptist college in a dry county of eastern Kentucky. It wasn't the typical college experience, but the school had quality soccer facilities and I liked the people on the team. Ultimately the offer was too good to turn down.

On September 11, 2001, I was a sophomore at Cumberland College living in the dormitory. My dorm consisted of a four-bedroom suite with a shared living room. Three of my soccer teammates lived in the suite with me. I remember sitting in the suite, watching the attacks with my teammates and thinking, *This is going to change everything, but I don't know how it's going to change my life*. But even after the tragic incidents of 9/11, I didn't have the immediate urge to join the military. I make the distinction because for many people with whom I later served, the events of 9/11 propelled them to military service. But for me, I continued thinking, *I've got to graduate college because that's what I'm supposed to do*.

After two seasons of soccer, I transferred to the University of Cincinnati (UC) in my hometown. I had enjoyed my time at Cumberland, but I was convinced that Cumberland didn't fulfill my need for a fun college experience. I knew that NCAA required a player to sit out a season after transferring schools. The thought of practicing with the team my entire junior year without guaranteed playing time my senior season seemed like a bad investment of my time. Said another way, once I transferred to UC, it was the end of my soccer career.

At UC I majored in accounting because of the mentorship from my grandfather Gilbert Scheller. I always looked up to him. He was the only military member I had in my family. He served in World War II and had landed on the beaches of Normandy. Following the war, he got out of the Army, went to Indiana University, and received a master's degree in accounting, which he used to get a job with the FBI. After years with the FBI, he later became chief federal probation and parole officer for the State of Illinois. I admired him tremendously. He told me, "Go get your certified public accountant credential, and you'll get a job in the FBI." That was my goal. I never really asked myself if I enjoyed accounting. I viewed it as a means to the life I wanted. I was always an aggressive guy. I didn't see myself sitting at a desk. In my mind I was going to go be an FBI agent keeping Americans safe from domestic threats.

My senior year in college, on a Christmas cruise with my family, I met girl named Jackie, who would later become my wife. I was twenty-two years old at the time. By the end of my senior year of college, she became a trusted friend and confidant as I went through changes in my life.

Transferring to UC gave me the "college experience" I was looking for, but I was ready to leave Cincinnati when I graduated. I wasn't in a fraternity, but the same group of friends from high school and college always seemed to be at our three-story college house partying and sleeping over. I needed to get away. I received some job offers in Cincinnati post college, but none of them lived up to the false promises fed to my generation. We were all told, "Go to college and you'll get a great job." As it turned out, there were no $80,000 jobs waiting for me, and $30,000 offers from subpar firms were not appealing enough to keep me in Cincinnati.

With only a college degree and $8,000 I had saved from working part-time, I decided to find a job on the East Coast. I literally packed all my stuff in a U-Haul and drove to Jackie's hometown of Virginia Beach. With the little bit of money saved in the bank and a dad who agreed to co-sign on a house, I secured a mortgage on a small townhouse in Norfolk, Virginia. Jackie moved in with me, and we began our life together.

After arriving to Virginia Beach, I got a job as an accountant at an auto manufacturing firm while Jackie finished her senior year at Old Dominion University. I enjoyed the freedom of owning my own house, but my job was unfulfilling and monotonous. I did basic bookkeeping that easily could have been accomplished with a seventh-grade math level. Even though I had an accounting degree, I never attained the CPA credential. After I moved, I realized Virginia required additional accounting classes for eligibility to sit for the CPA exam. It felt like a detail I should have been prepared for when I left Ohio as a degreed accountant. Conflicted about paying for more accounting classes to continue pursuing the accounting credential, I opted to fill my evenings with a second job delivering pizzas.

One night while delivering pizza to a group of college kids, I was invited into the apartment to chug a beer. Seeking a bigger tip, I agreed. But as I walked away, I felt a deep feeling of discontentment. My discontent didn't stem from the moral or ethical problems I probably should have experienced as a professional driver drinking beer on the job. My discontent was deeper. I realized this wasn't the life I envisioned. The move to Virginia Beach didn't provide the fulfillment I thought might be waiting on the East Coast. I had a nice townhouse near the beach and a path to a steady and safe career, but I found myself struggling with an energy that got more restless every day.

A week later at my accounting job, while pretending to file papers, I stared at a TV hanging in my office. It was autumn of 2004, and the Marines surrounded the city of Fallujah, Iraq. The newscasters spelled out the pending threat and combat awaiting the Marines over the next month. In that moment I felt ashamed

I hadn't done more with my life. That was the moment I knew I wanted to serve my country. It wasn't watching coverage of September 11. It was three years later watching the Marines on TV, which happened to coincide with a moment in time when I needed a larger purpose. God has a funny way of placing signs in your life when you need them the most. Watching the Marines in Fallujah, I thought, *Those individuals will always know they made a difference in this world.* I sought out the Marine recruiter the following week.

People often ask me why the Marines. I cannot answer that question definitively. My high school soccer coach was a Marine officer who always told me I would make a good Marine officer. Perhaps he planted a seed. Ultimately when I saw the Marines on the television in 2004, somewhere in my mind, I concluded the Marines were the best. My mentality was, *I want to go for the best, so I want to go for the Marines.*

At that time, it was still only one year after the United States invaded Iraq. Back then I was young and ignorant. Like many others, I was quickly convinced America needed to impose its national will on foreign lands. I lacked the life perspective and education required for a higher level of critical thought. I loved America, but I did not truly comprehend how to improve the country's sources of national power. It wasn't until I got older that I realized nationalism, patriotism, and the desire to serve can often be manipulated by leaders with alternative motives.

I am also embarrassed at the impact Hollywood movies probably had on my perspective. As an adolescent, I watched the movie *Black Hawk Down* over and over. That movie always made me want to pick up a gun and jump into the fight with the American warriors in Somalia. The movie glorified combat. But when I went back and studied the operational failures leading to that event, I realized it's a case study in poor decision making at the senior military and political leadership level. The senior leaders made terrible decisions at the operational level that led to numerous unnecessary casualties. But I couldn't see that back then. When I watched the movie as a college student, it epitomized heroism. It resonated with me as the embodiment of what it meant to be American.

I eventually met with my Marine Corps officer recruiter, Captain Martin, in Richmond Virginia. We talked for about an hour. At one point he said, "Marine officers serve a higher purpose." This spoke to me. That's exactly what I wanted. He gave me a recommended workout plan and a huge packet to fill out. I went home and immediately began chipping away. I had clearly gained some weight moonlighting in the pizza career field, so my first couple of runs were brutal. But training my body for a sports season was familiar. I had the discipline to push through the discomfort.

The officer recruiting/application pipeline was tedious and time consuming. The application required every personal detail imaginable, multiple recommendations, and professional history. Up to that point in my life, it was hard to itemize accomplishments. I had earned a degree and played a couple seasons of college soccer, but beyond that, I didn't have anything setting myself apart. But undeterred, I filled out all the paperwork as if I were an accomplished professional. Acquiring the recommendations was the hardest part. I reached back to college professors who I'm sure didn't remember me and former part time bosses. I eventually collected the required number of recommendations and called my recruiter to set up another appointment.

The second time I met Captain Martin we sat down, and he reviewed the application. He pointed out potential problematic areas. As if trying to reassure me, Captain Martin said many people applied two or three times and that an applicant shouldn't be discouraged if they weren't selected. After preparing me for the worst, he took me outside and supervised the physical screening portion of the application. I did well on the physical portion. When I left the recruiter's office, despite my physical strengths, I did not feel good about my chances.

Despite my trepidation, after a few weeks the recruiter called me and told me that my application had been accepted. He told me I needed come back to the office for a final physical test and paperwork. During this visit, Captain Martin revealed for the first time that he was a pilot.

"Hey, do you want to be a pilot? I've got flight contracts for you."

Again, not knowing anything about the military, I replied, "No. I see myself leading people on the ground with a gun. Like an infantry officer or something."

"All right," he said. "Well I can offer you an open ground contract, but I can't guarantee infantry. You never know what you're going to get with an open ground contract, so I recommend you take the air contract. Plus, you get more money if you're a pilot."

"No, that's not what I want. I want to be on the ground."

That conversation led to my entrance into the Marine Corps on an open ground contract.

After the meeting with my recruiter, I drove back to Virginia Beach feeling triumphant for getting through the application process. But three days after getting back to work, Captain Martin called me again:

"I need you to come back up here and do another physical test."

"Why? I just did one three days ago."

"It turns out they need to be completed within thirty days of shipping out to Officer Candidate School."

"Well, didn't that rule apply three days ago? Why didn't you know that?"

Then he snapped at me, "Look, you want to be a Marine? This is what being a Marine is about!"

Funny enough, in that moment, I almost hung up and walked away from the whole process. I was bothered, maybe more than I should have been, that he didn't acknowledge his mistake. I didn't want to ask my boss for more time off work to go back to Richmond. I also didn't want to run the physical test again. But sometimes when you want something from the system, it doesn't make sense to dwell on the mistakes of your leaders. So, I took more time off work and redid the physical test without the recruiter ever admitting his mistake.

The previous story about the recruitment process illustrated a trend that plagued me through my career. I don't care when people make mistakes. When a leader makes a mistake, all I need is an acknowledgment: "I messed this up. I'm sorry, but I still need you to do this." When leaders try to cover up their mistake through deception or anger, I feel it marginalizes credibility of the entire system. Little did I know how important this theme would be moving forward in my career as a Marine.

CHAPTER 3:

I'M GOING TO BE AN INFANTRY OFFICER—
OFFICER CANDIDATE SCHOOL. THE BASIC
SCHOOL. INFANTRY OFFICER COURSE.

"Remember that it is the actions, and not the commission, that make the officer, and that there is more expected from him, than the title."

—George Washington to the officers of the
Virginia Regiment

My selection to the Marine Corps officer pipeline was excit-ing. I told all my friends and family. My big mouth probably prevented me from quitting Officer Candidate School during my low moments more than any other attribute. Being perceived as a failure was one of my biggest fears. As I celebrated the acceptance, I soon realized the holiday season of 2004 was a transitional time. My life was changing. I was excited to be on a path filled with purpose, but I still had many loose ends in my life that needed ad-dressed: I had to sell my townhouse, notify my current employers of my departure, and figure out what to do with my belongings. I also wanted my girlfriend on the new path, so despite being so young, I proposed on Christmas 2004. She said yes.

I travelled up to Quantico for Officer Candidate School (OCS) with my fiancé on a cold January day in 2005. OCS is a ten-week program that screens for leadership potential in officer candidates. The first three days are administrative in-processing. It was quite clear from the onset that I was lost and out of place.

During in-processing one afternoon, I found myself sitting at tables with all the other candidates in dead silence. My eyes wandered from face to face as I engaged people. "Where are you from?" "Play any sports?" "Girlfriend?" Some people answered, but everyone appeared reluctant. Eventually a sergeant approached me.

"Are you having a good time?" he asked. Demonstrating an inability to read the room, I ignorantly and sincerely responded, "Yeah, I'm having a great time." His face immediately signaled that I had answered incorrectly. Then he barked, "You want me to ensure you're not having a good time?" I apologized and said no. It was an important first lesson: shut the fuck up until you understand why no one else is speaking. I conformed to the room and kept quiet during the rest of the in-processing. I slowly realized through in-processing that a large portion of the candidates were previous enlisted Marines. This demographic appeared to inherently understand how to navigate the process. Lesson two, which I didn't learn quick enough: befriend and emulate people who know what they're doing. I soon realized how unprepared I was for the methods of the drill instructors.

Following in-processing, the formal day one at OCS is referred to as "pickup day." On my pickup day all the officer candidates piled into a small cafeteria-style room and sat while the staff formally introduced all the drill instructors. At a certain point during the introduction, the drill instructors all violently reacted off a key word. I quickly found myself staring in shock at intimidating men on top of our tables screaming at frightening octaves. When the initial shock faded, I realized the drill instructors were ordering us to sprint out of the cafeteria and form into lines. Everyone had their luggage with them at that point. Two bags each. They ordered my platoon, about sixty-five guys, to march toward a giant asphalt parking lot known as the parade deck.

The drill instructors rampaged across the deck screaming at us to tighten up the lines as we scurried with bags over our shoulders. Before we got to our living quarters, known as the squad bay, they stopped the march and ordered us to dump out all our belongings. The drill instructors then started kicking everyone's items around, intimidating and hazing the candidates. Suddenly they barked at us to pick everything back up and put it in our bags. When I looked around, it occurred to me that all the other candidates were prepared for the event. All their belongings were packed in Ziploc bags, as they had anticipated the drill instructors throwing our belongings everywhere. I seemed to be the only candidate unprepared. My pencils, pens, underwear, socks, and toiletries were scattered everywhere. Of course, the other sixty-four candidates retrieved their items much more quickly and were on their way to the squad bay.

As the platoon disappeared into the squad bay, I was left alone with the entire cadre of drill instructors. They quickly swarmed me. I tried picking up my stuff as quickly as possible, but the drill instructors seemed incensed. They crowded my space. At one point I was on my knees reaching between shins to pick up a razor. In that moment, I quickly learned lesson three: don't be last. As the drill instructors berated me, it was easy to question my motives about joining the Marine Corps. I finally retrieved all my items and shuffled past the drill instructors into the squad bay. It was quite evident within the first hour of pick-up day that I was the most lost candidate.

The Officer Candidate School platoon staff consists of four staff noncommissioned officer (SNCO) drill instructors and a captain platoon commander. The platoon staff's primary objective is screening the, on average, sixty-five candidates for leadership potential. For comparison, enlisted boot camp is ten weeks and about 95 percent make it through. For OCS, only about 65 percent make it through. The attrition rate at OCS occurs due to drop on requests (DOR), injury, or performance. Performance is documented in a formal training jacket by the platoon staff. When a candidate fails a task, objective, or test, the instructors document the shortfall with a "counseling." If the officer candidate racks up enough counselings, they are sent to a board chaired by a colonel. The colonel makes the final determination if the candidate should be dropped for performance or allowed a chance to continue training.

This point of reference is relevant for understanding where general officers begin their career. I've always felt the Marine Corps could be more effective in its screening process for officers. Leadership screening should be the main effort in any organization. The criticality of the process cannot be overstated. The Marine Corps conducts leadership screening through the recruitment and Officer Candidate School pipelines. Thus, when candidates arrive to Officer Candidate School, the Marine Corps only has ten weeks left to determine leadership potential.

I felt officer candidates needed to demonstrate a balance between discipline and creativity. I felt the balance between discipline and creativity directly correlated to the balance of centralization and decentralization required on the battlefield. However, the process of Officer Candidate School heavily favored discipline. This was obvious based on the staff the Marine Corps assigned to screen at Officer Candidate School. While drill instructors had experience serving with officers, they had never been officers themselves. I wasn't convinced they were the best people to identify the qualities needed in officer candidates. The drill instructors relied on fear and intimidation to make easy tasks difficult. They taught through a herd mentality approach designed to weed out the weak. Most lessons were taught through repetition, repetition, repetition. My drill instructor's favorite stress-inducing technique, outside of screaming, was sleep deprivation. Every night we were expected to write multiple three-hundred-word essays for minor infractions during the day. Each essay robbed us of at least one hour of sleep.

Thus, the game became a test of resiliency. They wanted to determine if I could withstand the pressure and lack of sleep to remain disciplined in the easy tasks such as remembering to lock my footlocker or shave my face.

Resiliency is important for military leadership, but it always bothered me that critical thought wasn't emphasized more. A candidate could be a deep-thinking, geopolitical analyst with a bountiful knowledge of science, but he wouldn't make it through Officer Candidate School if he couldn't withstand beratement, yell programmed responses, and dance in a coordinated manner thirty inches behind another man.

My learning curve at Officer Candidate School was steep. After identifying from day one that I was behind, I quickly made strides to learn from my peers. My peers in the afterhours taught me things like how to stay out of sight from the drill instructors, how the rank structure worked, how to make a bed properly, and how to report. I always tried to show appreciation to my peers and prevent the extra help sessions from feeling burdensome. The relationships I developed were critical and ultimately directly illustrated my progression. There were three peer evaluations during the ten weeks when all the candidates ranked their peers based on perceived performance. Then each candidate was counseled by the drill instructor on their numerical ranking based on the peer evaluation. I was ranked in the bottom third during the first peer evaluation, but I moved up into the top third by my final peer evaluation. This metric, aside from commissioning, was probably my strongest indicator of development at Officer Candidate School.

Toward the end of my Officer Candidate School experience, my squad conducted a unit leadership evaluation. It was a twelve-mile unit run. We rotated leadership positions at each mile marker coinciding with a new station. The stations were a series of challenges mostly populated by instructors acting as enemy. It was a tool used by the captain to evaluate candidates. I started my station at the top of a hill. I led the squad to the base of the hill when a machine gun engaged us from the next hilltop. I evaluated the situation. All we had were M16s. I realized trying to charge the machine gun position was suicide. I felt the best course of action was to pull back, reassess, and figure out a different way. So, I screamed as loud as I could, "Retreat! Retreat! Follow me. Get back here." My instructor gave me feedback immediately following the station. "You had good command presence, but you screamed retreat. Marine officers never retreat."

"But, sir, we would have all died."

"Marine officers never retreat."

Reflecting back, I'm sure that captain was not an infantry officer. And I'm sure he only had four to six years of experience. But his statement stuck with me. It was a window into the culture of the Marine Corps. This was some of the best and worst advice I ever received.

In the end all that mattered was that I survived Officer Candidate School. I graduated and commissioned as a second lieutenant on March 25th, 2005. My fiancé and parents witnessed the commissioning. I can still remember the fulfillment I felt on that day.

Ten days later I checked into The Basic School. The Basic School is a process somewhat unique to the Marine Corps. In other branches, after commissioning, young officers report straight to their Military Occupational Specialty School. The Marine Corps uses The Basic School as an intermediate stop designed to develop (not screen) officers in their leadership, train provisional rifle platoon commanders, and determine military occupational specialty for ground contracts. It is a six-month program of instruction. It consists of numerous lectures, field training, and exams.

While there I trained with a platoon of fifty second lieutenants for the next six months. I lived with three other lieutenants in a cramped barracks room deemed livable despite the black mold problem that later condemned the building. Our training over the program of instruction was mostly facilitated by general support instructors. Over six months of basic leadership training, the staff impressed on me that I would soon find myself in Iraq. It often felt back then that Iraq validated Marines as professionals.

The leadership continuity throughout the instruction at The Basic School is the staff platoon commander. My staff platoon commander, Captain Ryan Gilchrist, was one of the best officers I ever worked with. He was an extremely intelligent infantry officer who also possessed people skills. He was also one of the few instructors at the time who had previously deployed to Iraq and experienced combat. He led by example and greatly influenced my career in more ways than one.

While training at The Basic School, my fiancé planned the wedding. After graduating college, she started a job at a public accounting firm in Richmond. Richmond was closer than Virginia Beach, but I was so busy that I still didn't have much time to help her plan the wedding. I was only able to visit on weekends, and even weekends weren't always reliable. The weekend of our scheduled cake tasting, I called Jackie and cancelled when I realized my land navigation failure required remediation over the weekend. She was not as sympathetic as I had hoped. And the weekends when I did visit, I was usually exhausted. One Friday I drove to see her after a weeklong field event. I was in such a hurry I didn't take the time to wash the cammie paint off my face. Speeding down to see her late Friday night, I was pulled over by a police officer. When the officer walked up, he found a worn-out Marine with cammie paint still on his face. The officer took pity on me that night and let me go. Jackie and I were both adjusting to how the stress of a Marine Corps lifestyle impacted a relationship. Eventually, we picked the Columbus Day weekend in October 2005 for our wedding. The date stood out because we knew the Marine Corps would likely give us at least three days off for the federal holiday weekend.

During occupational specialty selection time at The Basic School, all officers are expected to rank their career choices. The staff then decides, based on the lieutenant's preferences and the needs of the Marine Corps, how to divvy up occupational specialties. When it came time to rank my top choices, I listed intelligence officer and combat engineer ahead of infantry officer. When my staff platoon commander, Captain Gilchrist, saw my list of occupational specialty choices, he shook his head and said, "Scheller, you're going to be a fucking infantry officer. I'm not going to even entertain these other two choices." I thought he was joking. But when the formal occupational specialties were assigned, he called me into his office, stared at me, and said, "Infantry officer. I wasn't joking. It's the best fit for you. You would never be happy as an intelligence officer or any other career field." His conviction and faith in my ability to be an infantry officer was inspiring. Looking back, he was exactly right. I would have never made it in the Marine Corps very long with any other occupational specialty. Infantry officer was by far the best choice for me, but I lacked perspective at that time. I was fortunate to have a leader who understood my strengths, believed in me, and had the courage to tell me something at the time I didn't want to hear.

I completed The Basic School at the beginning of October 2005 and immediately started Infantry Officer Course. My wedding weekend was right around the corner, but I couldn't focus on the wedding. For Infantry Officer Course admission, I needed to pass the Combat Endurance Test. The test was a combination of a sixteen-mile run, land navigation, obstacle/endurance courses, and various other stations. At each station we were required to complete a task. We needed a certain cumulative time to pass the event. Failing tasks at the stations resulted in time penalties. I started the event strong. All my weekend land navigation remediations allowed me to find my locations rather quickly. But at about the eleventh mile I found myself at a ground fighting station. At the station, I met Captain Marcus Mainz for the first time, who I later realized was a college wrestler. Captain Mainz manhandled me. At one point he elbowed me in the eye, causing my eye to immediately swell shut. I walked away from that station feeling mentally defeated, but I didn't quit. I ended up finishing the event in the top ten of my seventy-man class despite only having one eye. I was overjoyed to pass the event. But my wife didn't appreciate my very noticeable black eye in all our wedding pictures.

I finally started to feel like I belonged within the Marine Corps while at Infantry Officer Course. No more absurd drill instructor games. No more classes about trivial administrative work. Infantry Officer Course involved an exciting balance of physical toughness and mental agility. My peers in the Infantry Officer Course 1-06 class were from all over the United States, but it was clear that we all wanted the opportunity to lead Marines in combat. This common goal, in conjunction with the suffering we endured over the next three months of the course, created relationships that lasted a career.

I had amazing mentors in Infantry Officer Course impacting and elevating me not just in terms of my career but also as a professional warfighter. Captain Marcus Mainz is someone I always admired. He epitomized the warrior poet I wanted to become. Marcus Mainz went on to become a battalion commander and was fired based on political correctness and equal opportunity allegations. During his battalion command, his ability to innovate and push his unit toward a warfighting culture was unparalleled. Another superior instructor in my Infantry Officer Course was Captain Brian Chantosh. This young captain had a Silver Star, but when reading his citation, it's clear he should have received the Medal of Honor for his actions. Unfortunately for him, his combat experiences occurred when the Defense Department didn't want to give out the Medal of Honor for fear the wars would appear more problematic than Secretary Rumsfeld and President Bush projected. Captain Chantosh exemplified a warfighter who didn't fit through the career advancement choke points. The bureaucracy forces officers to demonstrate a blend of political correctness, sales ability, office skills, and commandership. A superior commander lacking staff officer skills ultimately watches his career die in front of PowerPoint. Talent management should require identifying superior warfighting commanders, and protecting, developing, and focusing them. But instead, senior leaders interpret talent management as allowing demonstrated performers access through the narrow career path to well roundedness. The culture celebrates mediocracy. If Napoléon were in the American military today and he maintained a focus on warfighting and commandership at the expense of annual training, reviewing awards, or building PowerPoints, he wouldn't make it past O-5.

One of the final events we had before completing infantry officer course was a bonfire. During the event, General Mattis came to speak to my class around the fire while we all drank beer. He was only a two-star general back then. He arrived in a black suburban with a security detail. He also had a model girlfriend accompany him. Words can't describe how uncomfortable she made the group. There was no physical affection, or even affectionate looks, exchanged between the two. She was clearly there projected as a girlfriend and not some type of assistant. She stood off to the side in an uncomfortable manner that signaled something was off. I tried to ignore the awkwardness of the scene and focus on General Mattis's words. He told us that there was nothing better in the world than being a Marine. And that being a Marine infantry officer was a special responsibility. He told us something very similar I've seen him publicly say before, "The first time you blow someone away is not an insignificant event. There are some assholes in the world that just need to be shot." Then he elaborated, "There are hunters, and there are victims. By your discipline, cunning, obedience, and alertness, you will decide if you are a hunter or a victim. It's really a hell of a lot of fun. You're gonna have a blast out there. And I feel sorry for every son of a bitch that doesn't get to serve with you." At the time I remember being struck by General Mattis's presence and motivation. He fired me up to get to my unit. I only wish I knew then what I know now. I missed an opportunity in an informal setting to ask about counterinsurgency's effectiveness. To this day he has never commented on his failures as a theater commander in Iraq or Afghanistan.

CHAPTER 4:

IS THIS HOW COUNTERINSURGENCY WORKS?—
BEIRUT. RAMADI. FRUSTRATIONS.

"To make war upon rebellion is messy and slow, like eating soup with a knife."

—T. E. Lawrence

As my training at IOC neared completion in December 2005, I was assigned my first unit. Ironically, I was assigned to 1st Battalion, 8th Marines (1/8), the same unit I watched on TV in Fallujah. With the new orders, I needed to move from Quantico, Virginia to Jacksonville, North Carolina. According to Marine Corps regulation, we all deserved thirty days of leave (vacation) to move our personal belongings from duty station to duty station. I was looking forward to spending some of the transit time with my wife over the Christmas holiday. However, my new unit's battalion executive officer drove up to Infantry Officer Course so that he could personally deliver a message to me and my seven peers with orders to the unit. He told us how excited the leadership was to receive their new platoon commanders. He told us how important we were. And then he threatened us. "If any of you try to take the thirty days of leave, I will assign you to the battalion staff for the next deployment. If you want to be a platoon commander, I need you checked into the unit yesterday."

The 1/8 executive officer went on to tell us that the battalion was deploying in June 2006 on the 24th Marine Expeditionary Unit (MEU). For context, a MEU consists of a battalion (roughly a thousand Marines) embarked on three large Navy ships. A MEU is designed to be a theater reserve. But during a time of war, MEUs typically reinforce the war effort. Our battalion executive officer told us the MEU was taking us straight to Kuwait so that we could push north into Iraq. He also told us that 1/8's deployment preparations included training at an Army Base known as A.P. Hill in January. Hence why 1/8 needed us so quickly. The leadership wanted us checked in with our units prior to the holiday so that we could train at A.P. Hill as soon as the Marines returned from Christmas leave.

The excitement of finally getting to an operational unit overshadowed the cancelled time off. The only hard part was telling my wife who planned on spending our first married Christmas holiday together. Again, we were realizing together the toll a military lifestyle had on a family. Once I understood my follow-on duty station and a tentative timeline of the next few years, I told my wife to remain in Richmond with her current career. I didn't think it made sense for her to quit her new job and move down to North Carolina if I wasn't going to be around. Despite the obvious separation, I reassured her by stating that we were only four hours apart and we would still see each other on weekends. I reminded her that it was the same thing we had done for the previous year, but I'm not sure if that strengthened or weakened my argument. My plan was to fulfill my initial contract and then transition out of the Marine Corps. At that time, I believed we would end up together in Richmond after my one tour of Marine Corps service.

It typically takes between twelve to twenty-four months for an officer to get through Officer Candidate School to The Basic

School to follow-on occupational school, and finally to an operational unit. A young officer usually stagnates in the gaps between the schools. It was abnormal for me to complete my basic training in eleven months. 1/8's immediate need for us even expedited my exit from Infantry Officer Course. All lieutenants with orders to 1/8 didn't even attend the Infantry Officer Course graduation. I came out of the field one week, turned in my weapon, packed all my items from my barracks room into my old Hyundai Sonata, grabbed my graduation certificate, and drove down to Camp Lejeune a week before Christmas in 2005. I checked into 1/8 and was assigned as the 1st platoon commander for Bravo Company.

There are certain points of my career that I'll never forget. Meeting my platoon for the first time was one of those significant events. It was even more surreal and personal because it was the same unit that I had watched push through Fallujah a year earlier on TV. I stood in front of the thirty Marines and told them what seemed appropriate for an initial speech from their new lieutenant, "Hey, I'm your platoon commander. I'm going to be your leader for the next deployment. I will never ask you to do something that I won't be willing to do myself. I will pass out a written list of expectations, but I understand that words are cheap. My work ethic and performance will set the standard. I plan to earn your trust." I then thanked them for their service and told them I looked forward to the opportunity to serve them. I studied the Marines' faces as I spoke. It occurred to me that this speech was obviously much more important to me than most of them. Some of them didn't seem to be paying attention at all. But there were a select few studying me as inquisitively as I was studying them. One thing that struck me during the conversation was that half of them were in sweatpants and sweatshirts, while the other half were in the appropriate camouflage uniform of the day. I was smart enough not to mention my uniform observation during my initial conversation. But after my speech I pulled my platoon sergeant aside and asked him why half our platoon didn't feel the need to be in the uniform

31

of the day. Up to that point he had been very professional. After I asked my question, I immediately recognized the look of contempt on his face. "They just returned from Fallujah, Iraq, sir. Half of them still have shrapnel in their bodies. The doctor gave them light duty chits stating not to wear cammies because they shouldn't wear boots or restrictive apparel."

Words can't describe the embarrassment, reality, and fear that gripped me in that moment. The weight of my new responsibility enveloped me. I nodded to my platoon sergeant acknowledging my ignorance and watched as he walked away. I knew I had to work on building the trust of my men. I vowed to myself that I would do everything within my capability as a leader to ensure my Marines were prepared mentally and physically for any type of violent conflict.

A week after Christmas, I found myself in an aggressive work-up training cycle for Iraq. We began at Fort A.P. Hill, where I finally had the opportunity to train my Marines as a young officer. I truly enjoyed it. There was one incident at Fort A.P. Hill worth discussing. Within the first week of arrival, as I walked from the store to my living container with a large drink in one hand, a bag of food in the other hand, and my rifle slung across my body, I ran into one of my Marines talking to another Marine. As I walked by, I said, "Hey, Kelly," and continued walking. Kelly yelled back as I continued walking, "Hey, sir, I'd like you to meet my father." So, I stopped and walked over to the Marines, and found myself face to face with Brigadier General John F. Kelly. General Kelly went on to be the south combatant commander and secretary of Homeland Security under President Trump. I had only been in the unit for a week at this point, so I didn't realize that one of my lance corporals had a general father. I quickly put down the items in my hands and went to parade rest. The general was kind and didn't seem like he wanted to intimidate his son's platoon leadership. He asked me some easy questions about our training and the morale of the men. At an obvious breaking point, I excused myself, and left Lance Corporal Kelly and his father.

Through the work-up I developed a unique relationship with Lance Corporal Robert Kelly. Not only did I take special notice after meeting his father, but I quickly came to find out he was an outstanding American. Lance Corporal Kelly was an assault-man who had completed the unit's previous deployment to Fallujah. And if his combat experience wasn't enough, he was also one of the few enlisted Marines at the time with a bachelor's degree. While this is very common now, during the initial parts of the war, it was much less common. Lance Corporal Kelly decided to enlist after 9/11 instead of following his father and brother's footsteps to become a Marine officer. General Kelly was a prior enlisted Marine, but after one tour he got out of the military and pursued college. Once he earned a degree, he came back in as an officer. I felt Lance Corporal Robert Kelly was different. He was in a hurry to get into the fight. At the time he was also studying for the LSATs with ambitions to become a lawyer. Thinking about life after my first tour, I found myself in the after-hours sharing LSAT study materials with Lance Corporal Kelly. Later in my career, the special relationship I developed with Lance Corporal Kelly impacted conversations I had with both him and his father.

As I developed relationships and learned the strengths of my platoon in 1/8, time moved quickly. We always seemed to train away from Camp Lejeune. We spent multiple months on Navy ships preparing for the deployment in addition to our training at Army bases. At that time though, I preferred training away from Camp Lejeune. When we did stay at Camp Lejeune, on the week-nights when I wasn't in Richmond with my wife, I was relegated to my dilapidated apartment. I preferred living with the Marines in the field. As the training progressed, my battalion leadership continued communicating that we would sail straight to Kuwait and then insert into an Iraq battlespace. During early 2006, Iraq was a very violent and kinetic fight. Foreign fighters from all over the Middle East swarmed Iraq like a bug lamp.

We deployed in June 2006. My company embarked on the USS *Whidbey Island*. I shared a small room with two other platoon commanders. As soon as we departed Norfolk, we sailed across the Atlantic, through the Suez Canal, and headed straight for Kuwait. During the transit, I studied maps of Ramadi and Fallujah that I kept in my room. I built vignettes and tactical decision games over the maps to familiarize my platoon with the possible areas we could deploy. I also spent time reading Kilcullen, Mattis, and the small wars journals. I prepared my mind for counterinsurgency on the tactical level. At that time, I never questioned the macro utility of the counterinsurgency warfighting philosophy.

Even though we were very prepared for Iraq, as military history demonstrates, it is very difficult to predict and prepare for the next conflict. The real metric of success for any military unit is adaptability. A week before our ships arrived in Kuwait, an unexpected conflict broke out between Israel and Lebanon. Our naval ships turned around, and we sailed back toward Lebanon. As a platoon commander, I quickly filed away my maps of Iraq and began familiarizing myself with maps of Beirut.

Once our ships got within ten miles of Lebanon's coast, we launched a platoon to secure the embassy in Beirut. Then we pulled the ships up to a Lebanese port, where the crowds of Americans waited for us to board our ships. We sent Marines ashore to help control the embarkation of the citizens and then ultimately loaded the ships with as many citizens as possible. When we hit capacity, we drove the ships to Cyprus, where we dropped the citizens off. The ships moved back and forth between Lebanon and Cyprus multiple times. Every Marine and sailor lost their bed during the transit to Cyprus so that the civilians had a bed space.

I remember during one of the trips I was standing on the top deck of the ship and found myself speaking to a girl who appeared to be my age. She was very beautiful. I found out that she was a Lebanese-American dual citizen. She was a Harvard student who was back in Lebanon with her family for the summer. She thanked me profusely for what we had done to save her and her family. Not feeling like I personally had done much, I did my best to deflect the compliment. But she persisted. Somehow, she got me to reveal disappointment that the evacuation would most likely prevent me from getting to Iraq. When I conveyed this thought process, she studied me as if I was a creature she had never met before. It was clear to both of us that we saw the world through very different eyes. Finally, she told me I was a hero to her and that somehow she believed there would be other opportunities for leadership even if it wasn't in combat. Then we parted ways, and I never saw her again. On a spiritual level, it felt like a moment when Americans of different perspectives developed a deep connection of respect and love for each other through the bonds of our national values. Reflecting on the significance of that evacuation operation, the Department of State reported over the months of July and August of 2006 more than fifteen thousand Americans were evacuated. It was one of the largest noncombatant evacuations conducted by the United States until the Afghanistan evacuation in August 2021.

During the Beirut evacuation, everyone found it ironic that the 1/8's call sign was the Beirut Battalion. The call sign predated our 2006 Beirut operation. Sadly, 1/8 was the unit attacked with a vehicle bomb in Beirut in 1983, killing over 240 Marines. Those Marines in 1983 were also deployed on the 24th MEU, except back then it was called the 24th MAU (A for amphibious instead of E for expeditionary). Despite the respect I had for that generation, I always felt it was wrong to name a unit based on such a monumental failure. Senior leaders should have named the unit after the success of the Fallujah Operation. It also bothered me that senior leaders were never held accountable for placing Marines in the terrible position of Beirut circa '83. The colonel in charge of that MEU was a man named Tim Geraghty. Tim ended up writing a book and speaking on tour later in life. I had the opportunity to listen to him speak at my next duty station. By that time, he was very old, and his speech was well rehearsed. He clearly articulated the dynamic and challenging situation his senior military and political leaders placed upon him. I learned a lot. At the end he allowed an opportunity for questions. Coming off my first tour with 1/8, I felt obligated to ask, "Can you describe the barrier plan, trigger lines, and force protection plan you developed for a potential vehicle-borne IED?" He didn't get flustered at all by my question, almost as if there was always someone in the crowd who asked this type of insensitive question. He looked at me and said, "I couldn't control the decisions made placing us in that impossible position. I followed my orders in the manner I thought provided the best result. But I failed ensuring we had adequate security measures. The cars drove up to our perimeter unabated."

After the 2006 evacuation of Beirut, our ships stagnated off the coast of Lebanon for almost two months before they finally released us. I still remember the MEU commander, Colonel Ron Johnson, flying over to our ship to break the news. All the Marines piled into the bottom of the ship and looked at him standing on an armored vehicle as he gave his speech. "You did a great job on the evacuation. Only three months left in the deployment. Are you getting excited to go home?" The whole crowd cheered. And then after soliciting the desired response, the colonel screamed, "Well don't! We are going to Iraq! Get your heads out of your asses!" Colonel Johnson picked up the crowd's spirits intentionally so he could crush the crowd's spirits. He was always a derisive personality. Years later he would go on to be promoted to general only to be caught in an adulterous relationship with a young woman from a contracting company. General Joseph F. Dunford, the future commandant and chairman of the Joint Chiefs, sat him down and asked him to submit his retirement so that he could quietly retire with a full pension and an honorable discharge.

After Colonel Johnson's (un)motivating speech, our ships eventually landed in Kuwait. Once we debarked and started training in the desert, it seemed likely that we would push north. But that's not what happened. Based on the limited time left in our deployment they decided to put us back on ship and send us home. We were all very disappointed. The only Marines from our unit who got the opportunity to push north were our snipers. For context, in 2006 in the Al Anbar Province of Iraq, snipers were the main combatants. Snipers were getting killed on both sides, and our snipers were desperately needed to reinforce the fight. While our ships sailed back to Camp Lejeune, we received word that two of our snipers had been killed. Once we returned from deployment, as a young lieutenant whose goal was fighting in Iraq, I was filled with mixed emotions as I sat in my unit's memorial service for the killed snipers.

The unit quickly reset for the next deployment after returning from the MEU deployment. We arrived back to the United States in December 2006 and were immediately told our next deployment was in seven months. We were allowed two weeks for post-deployment leave, and upon completion the unit would start preparing for Ramadi, Iraq. My wife came down to Camp Lejeune for my post-deployment leave. During that time, she informed me of life changing decisions. She decided to quit her job and move down to North Carolina to be with me. I tried protesting and pointing out our quick deployment timeline. I reminded her of my plan to exit the Marine Corps after my second deployment. "I thought you were going to keep your job and I was moving up with you in Richmond after my next deployment," I asked puzzled. But she was convinced. "All of my peers at work think our marriage is a joke. No one understands. If we want this marriage to work, I need to come down and be with you." I couldn't argue with her.

By January 2007, all the company commanders switched out, and we immediately started the next work-up. I was asked if I wanted to be an executive officer or platoon commander in Weapons Company, but all I wanted to do was be a platoon commander in a Rifle Company for our Ramadi deployment. I lobbied to stay a rifle platoon commander, and initially the command obliged my request.

On the way home from my first deployment, I had requested a school seat to Winter Mountain Leaders Course. It was a three-month school from mid-January to the end of March. At the time when I put my name in for the school, I thought my wife would still be living in Richmond. But when I got my new company commander, he informed me that my name was pulled from the course because he needed me as a senior platoon commander to help train the company as we prepared our work-up. I didn't protest since it simplified my personal life with my wife moving down. Thus, my wife and I put in an offer on a house as soon as I returned from deployment and closed mid-January.

It was a Tuesday in January 2007. That weekend I had planned on moving all my wife's belongings out of her Richmond apartment and into our new house in North Carolina. That day my company commander pulled me into his office and said, "Hey, Stu, you know how I told you that you weren't going to Winter Mountain Leaders Course? Well, they never actually took your name off the list. It turns out that you're still going to need to go."

"Sir, what are you talking about? I just closed on a house. I'm moving my wife down to the house this weekend. When do I leave?"

"Thursday."

"You got to be kidding me, sir. You can't treat people like this."

"I'm sorry. I argued for you. But there's nothing we can do."

I was furious. I waited until 6:00 p.m. for my company commander to leave work. Then I walked up to the command deck and spoke with the operations officer, Major Kahn.

For a second lieutenant to go up and talk to the operations officer was very abnormal. But I felt I was being mistreated, and he was the person to address. I knew the operations officer was the senior officer in charge of school submissions. Since we had just returned from deployment, Major Khan was conducting a turnover with a senior captain. The senior captain, Captain Harbor, was sitting outside the office, and I walked right past him and into the major's office.

"Hey, sir, Second Lieutenant Scheller, can I have a moment of your time?" He motioned to the chair for me to sit. "I just want to talk about Winter Mountain Leaders Course. I was told that I wasn't going to the school, so I bought a house and planned on moving my wife down this weekend."

"Well here's the deal. We submitted a bunch of names for schools and people are dropping out all over the place, and it makes the unit look bad. We can't afford anymore school drops. We need you to attend the school."

"It sounds you guys didn't manage this correctly."

My reply was slightly disrespectful. He flipped the switch and started screaming, "Don't you come in my office and talk to me like that! We're going to Iraq. You need to get your mind right. You need to get ready for combat!" It was the same way my recruiter Captain Martin handled his mistake: deflection, anger, and blame.

I didn't back down. I looked at him and said, "How is going to Winter Mountain Leaders Course preparing for Iraq?" Then we had this awkward moment. Rather than give him time to formulate a clever last word, I stood up and walked out of his office. I remember when I walked out, I stared at Captain Harbor sitting outside the office. After listening to the whole conversation, he was wide-eyed with shock. To this day I'm not sure if his expression was a result of my behavior or how I was being treated.

That night I drove all the way up to Richmond because I wanted to tell my wife the news face-to-face. I didn't get there until about 1:00 or 2:00 in the morning to break the news. She cried. She knew once I got back from Winter Mountain Leaders it would be March. And from there I would head to Fort Pickett for a month and then to the Mojave Desert for another two-month training exercise. Then I would deploy for seven months. She had just quit her job and was justifiably upset. To make matters worse, she couldn't move all the furniture out of the apartment by herself. That night I got about an hour of sleep before my company executive officer started calling me wondering why I wasn't at work.

"Stu, where are you at? Why aren't you at work?"

"I'm in fucking Richmond, Virginia."

"The company commander is really pissed. He heard you spoke to the battalion operations officer last night. The operations officer said you were slightly disrespectful."

"Yeah. I did. And yeah, I was."

"Well, the company commander wants you in his office now."

"Well, that's not going to happen. I'm up in Richmond. I'll get there when I get there." I got off the phone, kissed my wife goodbye, and drove back down to Camp Lejeune. My company commander pulled me in his office as soon as I returned. He put me at the position of attention and berated me for going behind his back and talking to the operations officer. He told me I made the company look bad. I didn't respond. I let my face do the talking. When he was done yelling, I left the office, packed my bags, and got on the plane the next morning.

Winter Mountain Leaders was a challenging three months of training, but it had nothing to do with Iraq. When I graduated the course as a second lieutenant, the commanding officer of the school gave me a certificate and commented, "What a great way to start your career." I remember being slightly insulted because in my head I was already a one-deployment veteran.

When I returned to 1/8, the new platoon commanders had already checked into the unit. One of my new fellow platoon commanders in Bravo Company was lieutenant named Dave Borden. We instantly became good friends. It was also clear when I returned to the unit that the new battalion commander had a dominating presence. His name was Lieutenant Colonel Mike Saleh. Everyone feared him. He had already fired two company commanders while I was at school, including the company commander who sent me to the school. Being "Fired" in the military means a service member is shuffled to a less important job with an adverse or low evaluation report. The low evaluation is really what makes promotion and continued advancement after being fired almost impossible. My battalion commander also began firing some of the lieutenants. One of the people he shuffled out the door was the Alpha Company executive officer. Despite my pleas to remain a platoon commander, I was quickly moved over to Alpha Company to fill the executive officer billet. Shortly after, I was promoted to first lieutenant and began the work-up for Iraq.

CRISIS OF COMMAND

My battalion commander was very difficult. He was always angry. At that time, the wearing of personal, protective equipment (PPE) seemed to be the most important thing to him. If he ever witnessed a Marine not wearing full PPE during a training exercise, he would verbally berate the leaders and expect that the Marine receive a 6105 formal negative counseling. If he caught it a second time, the leaders would be fired. He believed an officer's responsibility was to "ruthlessly enforce the standard." However, unconsciously, he developed cognitive pathways relegating his vision toward small items he felt implied a lack of discipline. His overemphasis on discipline crippled his ability to use critical thought or see the bigger picture. For example, I remember he always demanded Marines remain at eyeball defilade in the turrets of our gun trucks. This meant only the Marine's eyes and top portion of the head could be exposed outside the armor. But the HMMWVs (High Mobility Multipurpose Wheeled Vehicle, or Humvee) we trained with in Camp Lejeune didn't have turret shields, meaning there was a gap of at least two feet of protective height outside the turret hole on the top of the vehicle for "eyeball defilade." One day Lieutenant Colonel Saleh came out to our training event while I supervised the training. The Marines at the time conducted snap Vehicle Check Points (VCPs,) which was a vehicle check point conducted hastily. Watching the drill, my mind immediately noticed standoff issues from the wire to the machine guns. It was also clear the trucks were positioned in a way that didn't incorporate locking field of fire. As I processed the situation, Lieutenant Colonel Saleh walked over and started screaming at me. I assumed the ass chewing would be for the same things I noticed, but I quickly realized he was upset the Marines in the trucks weren't at eyeball defilade while positioned in the trucks. I tried explaining that they were at the appropriate height if a turret shield was on the HMMWV, but as soon as I started speaking, he cut me off and reiterated, "Eyeball defilade!" So, for that training evolution, our Marines literally trained in the HMMWVs with only their eyeballs poking out of the turret hole, completely unable to hold the machine gun, because that's what he thought eyeball defilade meant. We never discussed tactical employment of the snap VCP.

We deployed to Ramadi in September 2007. We replaced Second Battalion Fifth Marines (2/5) in the southwest part of Ramadi. My company took over a place called Joint Security Station (JSS) Iron. It was a fairly established forward operating base (FOB) at that point. In addition to the JSS Iron position, my company had two additional platoon outposts for controlling the company battlespace. For context, at that time, the operating environment in Ramadi was very dynamic. When 2/5 began their deployment in January 2007, Ramadi was like the Wild West. When HMMWVs drove on the road, cars inherently knew to get off the road. People were shooting everywhere. But right around the spring of '07, a movement started that the Marines referred to as the Al Anbar Awakening. Ultimately the fighting in Al Anbar from '04 to early '07 consisted mostly of foreign fighters from Iran and other places. The Al Anbar Awakening consisted of local Iraqi leaders coming to the realization that the foreign fighters in Iraq were not in the best interest of the Iraqi population. It was one of the success stories of counterinsurgency. Once local Iraqis stared driving out the foreign fighters, the daily shooting matches almost immediately dried up. When my unit 1/8 showed up to Ramadi, it was not the same fight as when 2/5 began their deployment.

My job as the company executive officer seemed to be the jack-of-all-trades. We had disbanded the weapons platoon and moved to a nonstandard four infantry platoon organization within the company, so I picked up the additional responsibility of company fire support leader. I also was expected to supervise the security of all the positions, account for all the serialized gear, and oversee the patrol schedule. Our guidance from higher-up was to always maintain two patrols out in the battlespace. It was less clear what we needed to accomplish on the patrols. Through conversations with my company commander and battalion leadership, though not said directly, I concluded that flooding the battlespace with consistent presence was more important than any other specific purpose.

I tried to get out on one patrol with a different squad leader each day if possible. It helped me build my situational awareness in the city and better understand the strengths and weaknesses of the squad leaders across the company. For dismounted patrols, the amount of PPE we wore at the time was ridiculous. In the one-hundred-degree heat, I was fully covered from my chin to my thighs with my vest. I also was required to wear gloves. No one seemed to care that I couldn't see out of my glasses because of the sweat. We weren't allowed to wear bandanas to collect the sweat or take off our T-shirts under our long-sleeve camouflage shirt, because that lacked discipline. But ironically there was less risk of a heat casualty on the dismounted patrols. When we took the HMMWVs, we had to keep the heater on to prevent the vehicles from overheating. As a matter of survival, we developed a security halt technique in our mounted patrols to exit the heated vehicles in order to take a knee in the cool one-hundred-degree heat. The Marine Corps eventually learned from our feedback and dramatically slimmed down the PPE requirement over the next decade. But my senior leaders at the time cared more about protecting us from the threat than they did allowing us the speed needed to close with the threat.

There was one patrol I vividly remember. As the company executive officer, I studied the faces of the high-profile enemies in our area of operations daily. I felt I understood the enemy faces probably better than most Marines in my unit. During one of the patrols, I recognized the face of a high-profile enemy. When the man saw the patrol, he slowly turned and walked away. I started running and yelled at him in my best Arabic to stop. Once he realized I was chasing, he went into a dead sprint. I lifted my gun and yelled in my best Arabic that if he didn't stop, I was going to shoot. He didn't listen, and I didn't shoot. You can't shoot a high-profile enemy in the back no matter how sure you are in that moment. So, I lowered my weapon after the hollow threat and chased him. He was wearing a man dress and sandals. I was wearing over a hundred pounds of gear. He jumped over a fence. I climbed the fence as fast as possible and fell on the other side like a sack of potatoes. After another one-hundred-meter sprint he climbed over a wall. When I got to the base of the wall, I realized it was impossible to catch him with all my gear. In my mind I thought, *You win. I can't keep up with all this gear. Hopefully we see each other again tomorrow.*

Another time-consuming responsibility for me during that deployment was my title of Iraqi Police liaison for our battlespace. This responsibility was as amorphous as the intent of our consistent patrols. I spent most of my time drinking chai, smoking cigarettes, and eating goat meat to engage with the Iraqi Police (IP). In this capacity I coordinated Marine patrols to follow the IPs where they occasionally drove us to old weapons and munition caches to build goodwill. These were the same Iraqis who had served in the Baath regime, so they knew where Saddam Hussein's government hid all the weapons in preparation for another conflict with Iran. Ultimately, the IPs uncovered their own stockpiles of weapons and munitions, claiming they belonged to the "enemy," and used them as a bartering tool, justifying the money America continued providing them. From a financial perspective, it was a terrible investment on our part. All the weapons the Iraqis "found" were in terrible shape. Additionally, the IPs also always needed diesel fuel to fill up the Ford F-250 trucks America provided. The diesel fuel issue was laughable. My battalion leadership ordered me to stop giving the IPs diesel fuel while at the same time ordering us to ensure IP presences in all our patrols. Obviously, the IPs couldn't drive if they didn't have gas. Thus, my battalion leadership looked the other way while we continued giving them diesel fuel. My leadership begrudgingly concluded it was more important to have an Iraqi Police presence on our patrols, even if it meant we weren't building a sustainable force. It was clear then that building a sustainable force through the eyes of the local population was never the focus.

It is also worth noting how we handled our feces. We built wooden rectangular bathroom stalls. We sat on plywood circles, and underneath the sitting platform was an iron barrel that collected the feces. Twice a day our corpsman would pull out the barrels, pour diesel fuel into the barrel, and burn the feces. After a few months, the smell of the burning feces and cigarette smoke reminded you of home. As the executive officer, I always felt bad my corpsman, Hospitalman Nik Nixon, burned the feces every day. There were some days I did it for him as a gesture of shared suffering. I personally poured the JP-8 into the cut barrels, lit the shit on fire, and stirred the turds. Within the same topic, I always hated shitting in our wooden porta-johns. Iraq had flies everywhere. The flies were obviously attracted to the barrels full of feces. So, when we went into the plywood bathrooms, the flies came out of the barrels and landed on our faces. It's very demoralizing to have a shit-fly land on your face. Every time I took a shit, I refused to open my mouth. My biggest fear on that deployment was getting one of the shit-flies in my mouth.

Halfway through the deployment my unit moved out of the city and down to a new operating base referred to as Suwa. It was slang for sewer because it was built near a local Iraqi sewage creek, but I felt the name was appropriate because it was also a piece of shit. At that point America had been at war for five years, and yet I found myself at a new FOB with no infrastructure. I ended up showering with baby wipes for the remainder of the deployment. In FOB Suwa, I lived in a forty-foot shipping container with bunk beds. My company commander and interpreter shared the living space with me. We never made it one night without getting awakened at least three times because somebody always needed one of the three of us. In hindsight, it was the stupidest living arrangement.

One day I organized a patrol to take me back to Camp Ramadi. I had a meeting with the battalion leadership to discuss the update of my Iraqi Police force. Back then all our mounted patrols consisted of three old up-armored HMMWVs. For this patrol, the patrol leader was the corporal squad leader. I was just a passenger getting a ride to our destination. The Marines were always excited when I needed a patrol back to Camp Ramadi. While I attended the meetings, they were afforded an opportunity to eat in a chow hall, take a shower, and buy more tobacco.

When we pulled up to the battalion headquarters building, my battalion commander was standing out front drinking coffee. As he watched the patrol approach, he decided the speed of the patrol in the camp area was too fast. He walked in front of the patrol and stopped the vehicles while yelling for the patrol leader. I watched as the young corporal got out of the vehicle and started to take an ass chewing. Even though I wasn't the patrol leader, I didn't feel right sitting idly by. I got out of my truck and made eye contact with the battalion commander. As soon as he saw me, he stopped yelling at the corporal and stormed over to me. I immediately went to parade rest and waited for his correction. He screamed, "You're going too fast. You were going too fast." As he continued to yell, I broke eye contact and looked down at the dirt. When I looked down, he perceived it as disrespect. Incensed he yelled, "Did you just roll your eyes at me?" I looked at him with a confused look, but before I could answer, he started jabbing a knife hand into my chest. The force of his jabs pushed me back and out of my parade rest position. At this point a crowd of people started watching us outside the battalion headquarter building. I watched him survey the crowd, and then look back at me and yell, "I could fire you right now. Do you want me to fire you right now?" I was at a loss for words. My reaction as a man was to respond with physical force to anyone attacking me. But all I could muster up was a feeble apology. Feeling he had made his point, he walked back in the battalion headquarter building. At that point I turned to my guys, coordinated a link-up time on the trucks, released them to the camp, and went into my meeting. During the meeting I saw my friend Dave Borden. He represented Bravo Company as the Iraqi Police liaison. We spoke for a

spent, the more effective my company would be portrayed. But no one at the time thought to ask the question, "How effective was that money we spent to achieve the goals of the campaign?" And if they did, that feedback wasn't provided to us on the tactical level.

At that time in Ramadi, I wasn't sleeping much. I was working eighteen-hour days. I didn't really agree with the mission. My friend had gotten blown up. Every time my battalion commander visited our FOB he berated me and the company commander. It seemed logical for me to exit the Marine Corps and move on to the next phase of my life. All the other lieutenants picked their follow-on assignments, and when they did, I declared, "I'm getting out. I'm not picking a follow-on assignment."

The follow-on assignment for an infantry officer is where we leave the infantry and go do something else, like an instructor or recruiter. Essentially any nondeployable job. The thought process is that these jobs are a break from the hours Marines work in operational units, but I would later realize that often we worked more hours in these follow-on assignments.

I called my wife from Iraq and told her my plans:

"Hey, I'm getting out."

"Well, when can you exit?"

"Probably in the summer."

"Well, what are you going to do?"

"I don't know. I don't have time to look at that. I had planned on moving up with you to Richmond. I'll figure something else out. My plan is simply to get out."

"Stu, I just quit my job. I just moved down to North Carolina, and we bought a house. You haven't spent more than a couple of weeks living in the house. Please take a nondeployable here in North Carolina, and then you can get out and we can figure out what we want to do next."

I took a couple days and thought about her logic. It was hard to argue. After talking to my wife, I concluded, *Maybe I'm just so worn out that this is not the best time to make huge life decisions.*

I talked to my company commander, with whom I had a good relationship, about the conversation with my wife. He counseled me to take a job at the School of Infantry East in North Carolina. It was close to my house. I would have an opportunity to be a company commander and lead basic Marines coming out of boot camp. It would be a break he told me. From that duty station I could decide what next to do with our lives.

As I was leaving Iraq, at the end of April 2008, there was an attack on an adjacent infantry battalion that epitomized the fight in Ramadi at that time. The unit 2/8 served adjacent to us for the whole deployment and was in the middle of conducting their relief with 1/9. On April 22, 2008, two Marines, Lance Corporal Jordan Haerter from 1/9 and Corporal Jonathan Yale from 2/8, sat at the entry checkpoint for the company FOB. The deployment for 2/8 was much like ours: small spats of firefights filled with large lulls of presence patrols and nation building. Within days of departing, Corporal Yale sat at the control point and showed Lance Corporal Haerter the procedures for the gate. The gate didn't have many Marines because it was mostly manned by a large contingent of Iraqi Police forces. Within an instant, a dump truck approached the control point at a high speed. It began aggressively pushing through the barrier system. The Iraqi Police all ran. The two Marines stood in the middle of the road and fired at the dump truck. The driver was shot and was forced to detonate the explosives in the control point, instantly killing himself and the two Marines. After the explosion, the Iraqis all told the story of the Marines' courage to the point that most people didn't believe them. But following the attack, a damaged security camera in the explosion actually still had the footage of the attack. General Kelly, who conducted the investigation following the attack, explained later that it was exactly as described. Two Marines who didn't know each other, while all the Iraqis fled, quickly grasped the gravity of the situation. They were willing to die next to each other as brothers if it meant saving all the other Marines on that FOB. As I digested the weight of that situation on my flight home from Ramadi, the actions of those two Marines filled me with love. I knew I had made the right choice to remain in the Marine Corps.

It also should be noted that my battalion commander was not promoted to the rank of colonel. His derisive leadership was well known by the leadership in Iraq and home station. So, he retired as a lieutenant colonel, where the institution in all its wisdom then hired him to teach at the Naval War College. He is still there today as I write this book, influencing the minds of all the future general officers.

CHAPTER 5:

POST TRAUMATIC WORK LIFE—
WALTER REED. LOST GEAR. KIDS.

"There is no such thing as work-life balance. Everything worth fighting for unbalances your life."

—Alain de Botton

When I returned from Ramadi, I immediately visited my friend Dave Borden at Walter Reed in Washington, DC. My wife, Jackie, accompanied me on the first trip. Dave was in bad shape when I first saw him. He had hundreds of ball bearings still in his body, and his leg was missing from below the knee. Looking at him in the bed, I was amazed that he had survived. He looked terrible. Dave ended up going through hundreds of surgeries the next year. I visited him when I could. The resiliency he demonstrated was amazing. Dave ended up recovering from the surgeries and was fitted with a prosthetic leg. But a year later he was still having trouble walking and ultimately asked the doctors to amputate his leg above the knee for a faster recovery. The doctors obliged, and my friend, over a year after the incident, went through another long road of recovery. Two and a half years after the incident, Dave Borden worked his way back into a deployable unit with a prosthetic leg. He later deployed to Afghanistan twice, once as a regimental headquarters company commander and again as a general's aide. Dave Borden is truly one of the greatest Americans and Marines I know. He ended up medically retiring as a major. I attended his retirement. I didn't see Dave again until he showed up to my court-martial to testify as a character witness.

After one of my visits to see Dave, I drove down I-95 South to Camp Lejeune and stopped at a restaurant in the familiar town of Quantico. Ironically, while there I ran into Lance Corporal Robert Kelly from 1/8, who was now Sergeant Kelly working as a Marine in Quantico. We were both in the restaurant alone, so we decided to sit and eat together. I was surprised to see Kelly was still in the Marine Corps. I always assumed he would go to law school after his 1/8 tour and all our LSAT studying. When I asked him about it, he admitted that he took the LSAT but decided that with the war going on in Afghanistan he still felt an obligation to his Marines. Instead of applying to law school, he was pursuing a Marine Corps officer application. I was stunned.

"Kelly, you are one of the few people who enlisted after 9/11 with a college degree. You fought in Fallujah in one of the most kinetic fights of our generation. You have nothing else to prove. Why would you want to go through a year of training to become an officer?"

"I love America. I love the Marine Corps. I love the Marines. And during war, our Marines need strong platoon commanders. I believe this is my purpose. Law school will always be there when I get older."

I was at a loss for words. When I left the restaurant that day, for the remainder of the drive home I couldn't stop thinking about the last two people I had spoken with. I had left the hospital bedside of one of my friends fighting for his life, which according to him was so that he could continue serving Marines as an officer. And then I had sat down and talked to a man who refused to cash in a winning hand so that he could continue serving the Marines. Part of me was filled with pride for knowing these men. The other part of me was left feeling inadequate. I felt like I had more to offer. That was the moment I started desiring to serve in Afghanistan. I continued to text and email Kelly after our chance run-in. In fact, I even wrote him a letter of recommendation for his officer package. But that day in the restaurant was the last time I would ever see him.

War takes a physical and mental toll. Veterans are not victims, but there are sensitive topics that could be discussed more often. Following my deployment to Iraq, about a week after seeing Dave and Kelly, I started experiencing some of my own medical issues. Ten days into my postdeployment leave, my arm went numb, and I experienced debilitating chest pain. I thought, *Shit, I'm having a heart attack*. On that day I managed to get myself in the car and drive to the emergency room. The doctors ran all the tests: EKGs, chest X-rays, you name it. Naturally, I expected to hear a diagnosis.

"No, you're healthy. You're great."

I was in disbelief. "That can't be right. You can't expect me to walk out of the hospital like nothing happened."

"Well, maybe you have PTSD."

"I don't have PTSD. I was not blown up. I didn't kill anyone. This is not PTSD. I know what PTSD is, and this is not it. I'm having real physical symptoms right now. I don't have bad dreams. I don't feel bad about anything."

At that time, PTSD (posttraumatic stress disorder) was a huge topic for service members returning from war. After listening to my argument, the doctors responded with, "Well after your time in the warzone, your fight-or-flight sympathetic nervous system can be overloaded. It may take a while for the body to adjust. You'll be fine; just give it time."

I never told my command as a young officer about all my struggles. According to the rules, I should have followed up with my military doctor after my emergency room visits, but I never did. I thought they would think less of me as an officer if I had medical problems. The Marine Corps has come a long way in its strides to destigmatize treatment following combat deployments. But the truth is, superiors can never separate your problems from their subjective evaluation of your performance. It's impossible in a system that solely relies on a boss's impression of an employee for performance. To say otherwise is false and only further exacerbates the distrust of the system.

I struggled with anxiety and still do to this day. The medical field did not fully comprehend my problems back then. I have experienced real physical symptoms of anxiety after some of my stressful deployments. But my underlying problems didn't fall neatly into the disorder category many professionals were familiar with. Unfortunately, it took me a while to figure it out.

Following the Ramadi deployment, it was refreshing and enjoyable living with my wife in our house. It finally felt like we were a married couple. At the time we had two dogs, and we were both young working professionals. She took a job auditing for a bank in Wilmington while I continued my career in the Marines. At that point, we hadn't spent enough time together to seriously consider children.

Later that summer of 2008 I checked out of 1/8 and checked into the School of Infantry East. I was assigned to Infantry Training Battalion East. Infantry Training Battalion was an interesting experience for a young officer. For context, new enlisted Marines go through ten weeks of boot camp. Following their boot camp, all of them go to the School of Infantry (SOI) to learn basic infantry skills. SOI has two main training pipelines. The first pipeline, Marine Combat Training (MCT) battalion, is for all enlisted Marines leaving boot camp with a MOS (military occupational specialty) other than infantry. The second pipeline, Infantry Training Battalion (ITB) is for all enlisted Marines leaving boot camp with an infantry MOS.

While I checked into ITB, a new lieutenant colonel assumed command of the battalion. His name was Lieutenant Colonel

Thomas Hobbs. He impacted my life tremendously and developed my leadership as a young officer more than any other mentor in my career. Lieutenant Colonel Hobbs was not the typical officer. He was a big Samoan who used the call sign Sumo. Most infantry officers were skinny, athletic white guys. I appreciated that he was different. He was a very distinguished and intelligent officer who had also served as the battalion executive officer in 3/8 during a deployment in Ramadi '05, which suffered a jaw-dropping number of casualties. He had previously been an instructor at The Basic School and at Expeditionary Warfare School. I admired everything about him.

My previous leadership examples between Colonel Johnson and Lieutenant Colonel Saleh established an abrasive and derisive baseline. Even though that wasn't my preferred leadership style, I found myself imitating their techniques of fear, intimidation, and rank/position as sources of power for my leadership style. It's like an abused child who recognizes the pain of mistreatment, but ironically still finds himself predisposed to abusive behavior later in life because of the unconscious learned behavior. At that point in my career, I just didn't have a role model who demonstrated how to use relationships, ideas, and charisma to effectively influence Marines. Lieutenant Colonel Hobbs was the first commander who demonstrated all the qualities that I wanted in a leader. He took me under his wing and mentored me on how to be more a compassionate and thoughtful leader. I absorbed a great deal from him. He was the leader I asked to promote me to captain. The same day as my promotion, Lieutenant Colonel Hobbs assigned me as his Echo Company commander.

For context, at that time, there were five companies within ITB training three hundred privates in two-month increments. All the companies were led by a captain. I was one of the five training company commanders. It's also helpful to realize during that time the Marine Corps was growing the force because of the wartime demands. The accelerated need for young Marines didn't allow for much down time between courses. Each company staff was afforded only a week of down time between cycles.

As a company commander at ITB, I tried focusing on the development of my instructors so that they could in turn provide the best training for our student population. In my company, I had roughly twenty enlisted Marines comprising my staff. I quickly realized that understanding the potential problems in the personal lives of my instructors was a full-time job. At that time—2009—all my instructors were on at least their second tour. All of them had just come off an Iraq or Afghanistan deployment. They all seemed to cope with their experiences with heavy drinking. The instructors' alcohol problem impacted our schedule on a weekly basis. It was also clear that they all had marriage problems. When analyzing the divorce problems in my instructor cadre, I came to realize that service members' spouses were willing to put marriage problems on the shelf during deployments. Almost all spouses wanted to support their service member, but they all had unspoken expectations for a return on investment from lost time. Spouses had misguided expectations when service members left operational units and took jobs at nondeployable billets like ITB. Unfortunately, we all realized together our job tempo at ITB, and other similar non-operational units dictated a work schedule that we referred to as "dark to dark." The instructors had very little time home. And in the limited time they did get off work, they used alcohol to decompress.

Almost every single one of the instructors went through a divorce while I was there. I proactively brought in chaplains and professional speakers. We also sent instructors to marriage retreats and inpatient alcohol treatment centers. It was a tough time. But despite all my efforts, I at best only had a marginal impact. Everyone struggled emotionally. Yet despite the obvious problems in my instructors' personal lives, what many Americans may not appreciate is that all my instructors were eager to get back to a combat zone. At the time I didn't fully understand the psychology. Not often acknowledged but understood by those who have been there, full-blown daily combat fades out all other problems. The warrior becomes completely present. All the marriage, money, and drinking problems cease to exist. Combine that present state of mind with a sense of important purpose and extreme team-building cohesion, and the emotional experience of combat becomes very hard to replicate. For many service members, facing another warrior in the arena of combat is one of the highest levels of consciousness.

At ITB we worked dark to dark because of how serious we took the responsibility of training young privates before they went off to war. Once the students left ITB, many of them ended up downrange in a war zone within four or five months. We all felt a moral obligation to ensure we offered the best training possible. But again, the moral obligation to our Marines came at a heavy cost to our personal lives.

Over the next six months, we trained and graduated three classes. During the end of the third cycle within my company, my staff identified something that sent me through one of the toughest ordeals of my career. While returning all the students' armory items at the end the of course, the armory provided my staff with paperwork claiming the company still owed five machine gun optics. The paperwork stated ten machine gun optics had been signed for by one of my corporals six weeks before, but my corporal only returned five of the ten. In other words, we had operated for six weeks thinking we had turned in all our machine gun optics, only to find out at the end of the class we were missing five. The situation immediately generated questions. Why would my staff only return half of the optics at the scheduled turn-in time without questions? Why didn't my company gunnery sergeant, Gunnery Sergeant Davis, check the paperwork when the corporal came back and said he turned in all the gear? Were the optics really lost, or was this an accounting error and/or forgery from the Marine working in the armory? After identifying the problem, we spent forty-eight hours going through every wall locker, vehicle, and sea bag. We looked everywhere. When the armory claimed it wasn't an accounting error, I concluded the serialized gear was missing and that it was unlikely we were going to find them.

The Marine Corps made it very clear from day one that an officer is always accountable. I wasn't supervising Gunnery Sergeant Davis's armory counts that class. The armory counts and paperwork were his responsibility according to his billet description. We were both on our third cycle of training students at that point, so neither of us had an excuse about how the system worked. Whenever someone's job is at risk, fear can drive actions if the individual is not careful. Part of my survival instinct made me want to bring attention to Gunny Davis's billet description. But I knew deep down that delegating authority wasn't the same thing as delegating responsibility. Plus, I truly cared for Gunnery Sergeant Davis. He had a finger shot off in Fallujah. He was struggling with some of the same personal problems as the rest of my instructors.

Over the forty-eight hours while the optics were missing, I didn't go home. I was sleeping a few hours a night on the couch in my office during the search. At 2:00 a.m. on the third day, I sat behind my computer at work and sent Lieutenant Colonel Hobbs, my battalion commander, an email. I started the email addressing seams between the armory and company that allowed the optics to go unaccounted for six weeks. I then outlined the extensive search for the optics to no avail. I then stressed my failures to supervise. Lieutenant Colonel Hobbs used to tell us that if we ever saw an injustice, we needed to be brave enough "to throw our rank on the table." That expression always stuck with me, and it was the same expression I used in my first video.

I concluded my email to Lieutenant Colonel Hobbs that night by saying, "My company gunny failed, but so did I. I am the commanding officer, so I am ultimately responsible. I just came off a Ramadi deployment where, as the executive officer, I accounted for millions of dollars of equipment across Iraq. I knew how the process should have worked, and I didn't properly train or supervise Gunny Davis. I am throwing my rank on the

Around 2009, the military was trying to dramatically draw down in Iraq. The commandant of the Marine Corps at the time was General James T. Conway. General Conway publicly stated that the Marine Corps was pivoting the force from Iraq to Afghanistan, ultimately concluding there was more of a fight in Afghanistan. Even though the Afghanistan war started before the Iraq war, General Conway effectively shifted the preponderance of the Marine Force to Afghanistan almost eight years after it began. Very quickly the Marine Corps narrative went from "You don't know anything because you haven't been to Iraq" to "You don't know anything because you haven't been to Afghanistan." Still young, I let this new narrative influence me more than I probably should have. The new narrative furthered my resolve to find a way into Afghanistan.

The path I found to Afghanistan was through an organization called Joint Improvised Explosive Device Defeat Organization (JIEDDO). I didn't know anything about the organization or what it meant for me in terms of the deployment, but my job placement professional told me, "You'll get to experience a lot of combat. You'll be moving with Explosive Ordnance Disposal (EOD) and Route Clearance Platoon (RCP). The only catch is that it's a year deployment. But the Marine Corps pledged to support the requirement with an infantry officer, and you'd be perfect."

I accepted the JIEDDO deployment to Afghanistan in February 2010, and my wife told me she was pregnant in April 2010. It felt like the cloud hanging over my head at ITB had finally moved. I had always wanted to be a father. It was one of the most exciting moments of my life. The excitement created mixed emotions with the pending deployment. I felt like my responsibility as a husband and father was to be there for the pregnancy and birth. But again, my wife was very supportive. She assured me she could handle the pregnancy with the help of her family.

Just before my deployment, my wife and I went crib shopping. We went to Wilmington and made a day of it. By the third store, I had seen more cribs than I felt necessary. While in Babies R Us, I found a crib I liked. "I want this crib."

"I'm going to keep looking," she said.

"Well, I'm just going to stay here by the one I like while you look around," I ignorantly and insensitively said.

She broke down crying. Not slow tears. Sobbing. Everyone in the store started looking at us. "You don't care enough to keep looking," she yelled between the sobs.

I tried apologizing, but there was no calming her down. I took her by the hand and led her out of the store while everyone stared at us as if I had just abused her. The drive back to our house was long and awkward. We ended up buying the crib online because we couldn't bring ourselves to go crib shopping again. I tell that story only to illustrate that even though my wife was supportive of the deployment, it doesn't mean the stress of an upcoming deployment doesn't take a mental, physical, and spiritual toll on a marriage.

When I checked out of SOI, Lieutenant Colonel Hobbs gave me my fitness report. He gave me the top company commander report. In my official file, it still shows he ranked me number two of the thirty-five total captains he had ever reviewed. This is verifiably true. He thought very highly of me, despite, or perhaps because of, the struggle we experienced together. I considered him like a father in many ways. That's why it was so hard for me mentally when he turned on me later.

I checked into JIEDDO in Crystal City, Virginia, just outside of DC. Other than some generic administrative paperwork and annual training required for the deployment, I received a three-day IED crash course from an old IED maker in the Hilton lobby. They disguised the name of the conference room and locked the door behind them. Ultimately, he taught us how to build a basic circuit and the creative ways to do so. He also gave us a rundown on the different types of homemade explosives.

Afterwards, JIEDDO bought me a plane ticket to Kuwait International and told me that my final destination was Task Force

Paladin headquarters at Bagram Air Base in Afghanistan. Task Force Paladin was the subset of JIEDDO in Afghanistan. They did not provide any other logistical coordinates. I flew commercial to Kuwait with three military checked bags. I was on my way to a year of combat that shaped my thinking on war in many ways.

CHAPTER 6:

WHY ARE WE STILL HERE?—
AFGHANISTAN. FLASH FLOOD. PAKISTAN.

"We will make no distinction between the terrorists who committed these acts and those who harbor them."

—President George W. Bush

When I boarded the plane to Afghanistan, I was told someone would be waiting for me in the Kuwait International Airport. I should have asked more questions. When I got off the plane I wandered around aimlessly, expecting someone to have a JIEDDO or TF Paladin sign. I obviously appeared lost. While I wandered around the airport some random American approached and asked if I was an American service member. At that point I was pushing a cart with three sea bags, or a year's worth of gear. "Yes" I said almost sarcastically looking at all my gear. Then he pointed and said, "Go over there and get on that bus." I tried to explain who I was and where I was going, but he cut me off and said, "If you're a service member without a unit, get on that bus." The next two weeks of travelling were more of the same. I kept expecting there to be some type of scrutiny on my travel plans, and it never happened. I continued to be told by some guy to get in another line as I traveled closer to my final destination via bus, plane, and helicopter. At each stop, no one ever asked to see my official orders. All they needed to know was where I was going, and if I had my military ID card.

I finally arrived at the TF Paladin headquarters on Bagram Air Base in Afghanistan. As soon as I arrived, I was struck by the size of Bagram. It was the biggest base in a combat zone I had ever witnessed. There was an air base in Iraq called Al Taqaddum, referred to by the Marines as TQ, which was the closest comparison I had from personal experience. But TQ didn't appear as crowded or as large as Bagram. For context, the main highway in Bagram was known as Route Disney. I dreaded Route Disney more than the routes I later travelled with multiple IEDs. Unfortunately, I needed to walk a half mile on Disney every day to eat at the chow hall. Travelling on Route Disney I saluted a couple hundred people each way. Why did we salute in a crowded area in a combat zone? Because someone lacked courage. Route Disney was also full of service members driving golf carts with reflective "glow belts" around their body. Why would a person need a glow belt while driving a vehicle with headlights? Because someone lacked courage. Many of the soldiers walked to the chow hall with a trash bag over their weapon to prevent from having to clean it later. Why would someone walk to the chow hall with a trash bag over their weapon? Because someone lacked courage. Off Route Disney were concert venues, ice cream parlors, coffee shops, fast food restaurants, stores, movie theaters, intermural sports fields, and arcades, just to name a few. Route Disney was a microcosm for the lack of courage in our organization as a whole and is an example of why the United States failed the war on all levels.

Senior military leaders had divided Afghanistan into regional commands (RCs), which allowed subordinate general officers to control a small piece of the fight. TF Paladin leadership assigned me to RC East. As a Marine officer, I was surprised to be assigned to RC East because at the time, all the Marines were fighting in RC South-West. I had assumed that's where TF Paladin would place me. The logic was explained to me by an Army lieutenant colonel, whose billet or name I can't remember but whose face and words I remember clearly. Reflecting back, I'm assuming he was the operations officer or deputy for Task Force Paladin in June 2010. He sat me down in his office and started a conversation by expressing clear disappointment that General Stanley McChrystal had just been fired. He felt McChrystal had clearly communicated a counterinsurgency strategy with an achievable endstate and that President Obama had undermined all their efforts. It was clear this lieutenant colonel had briefed the general, or at least the general's staff multiple times, and really believed in McChrystal. After the initial vent session about McChrystal, the lieutenant colonel then got out a map and described to me his understanding of the Afghanistan strategy.

"You see this circle? That's Highway 1. That's the ring route. The ring route is critical to the strategy. General McChrystal's goal was never to kill the Taliban in the corners of Afghanistan outside of the ring route. That's what the Marines don't get." The lieutenant colonel paused at that point to let it sink in that he was about to tell me more about the Marines. "General McChrystal created TF SW because the Marines couldn't integrate their assets effectively with the rest of the force. So McChrystal gave them Kandahar and Helmand Provinces because they are the furthest away from what's most important: Kabul. He knew the Marines wanted their next Iwo Jima, and he knew there was plenty of fighting in the small south-west corner of the bigger fight. The Marines are buying us time. They are doing great things, but I need you to understand what they don't seem to understand."

I felt like his attack on the president and then on my service branch was discrediting out of the gate. I wanted to write him off, but something about the way he spoke and carried himself made me want to listen to him. "I'm not sure I understand," I said.

"Where you're sending me, Paktika Province in RC East, it is still east of the ring route. And the ring route also goes through Kandahar and Helmand Provinces in RC SW. If the ring route is so important, then why don't we just make that the focus?"

"The fight is obviously larger than the ring route. The endstate is a sustainable central government. But the ring route is critical to accomplishing the endstate. We decided fighting the Taliban outside the ring route provides better standoff. If we control the key logistical highway, then the central government in Kabul has a chance. Why am I telling you this? Because as a CIED team leader, if the IEDs start making their way onto Highway 1, then you are failing."

"It seems to me that the different ethnicities and tribes of the Afghan people may never respond well to a central government. How long do we need to hold the ring route for this strategy to work?"

"I'm not sure. With General McChrystal being fired, we definitely took a step back. But our fight right now is buying time for the central government to build legitimacy."

"But this war is being fought under the banner of terrorism. This was never supposed to be about building a central government like Bush outlined in his intent for Iraq. Why do you think we are here?"

I realized before he spoke that I had made a mistake asking the question. The look of contempt and disgust was clearly visible all over his face. "Don't ask that question. Don't ever ask that question. Your job as a military officer is to perform within the context of the current fight. Can you do that?"

"Yes, sir. I understand."

"I assigned you to RC East because in my mind that's the main effort fight for the strategy. It borders Pakistan, and it's where all the IED-making materials and fighters are entering the battlespace. We need a smart infantry officer like you making a difference. You are going to support the 101st Airborne."

"OK, sir, I understand. I appreciate your time."

About nine meals, thirteen hundred salutes, one concert, and seven Green Beans coffees later, I started my travel from Bagram to RC East. I flew to a Battalion FOB in Paktika Province called Orgun. The battalion I was assigned to support from the 101st was 1-187. Orgun was their battalion headquarters.

When I arrived the first thing I did was meet the Army Explosive Ordnance Disposal (EOD) team who had operated in the area for a while. There was an EOD Army lieutenant, but it was clear the staff sergeant EOD team leader was the real leader and brains of the operation. The team was always on the go. They responded to IEDs all over the battlespace. Most of their responses required flying into small platoon outposts on the border followed by a dismounted patrol to the suspected IED. EOD's job was simple: render a potential IED safe. They typically did this by driving their robot up to the IED, placing a charge on the IED, and detonating the IED. If there were exploitable items in terms of biometrics (fingerprints, DNA, and so forth for the FBI database), we collected it after the fact. Only when the terrain prevented the robot from placing a charge did the EOD tech walk up to the IED in his bomb suit. Occasionally the EOD teams took long mounted patrols from the FOB to the company positions. Whenever there was a mounted patrol, they worked hand in hand with the Route Clearance Platoon (RCP).

The Route Clearance Platoons in RC East always seemed to be an Army National Guard engineer unit cross-trained stateside for the specific RCP mission. At Orgun, the RCP was a National Guard Unit out of South Dakota. I had never been to South Dakota, but I liked almost every single solider in that platoon. They had a strong lieutenant and a strong platoon sergeant. All the soldiers kept a positive attitude and were passionate about the importance of their job. Despite their positive attitude, there wasn't much doctrine on how to conduct RCP back then.

The strength of RCP came from the first two vehicles: a Husky and a Buffalo. The Husky was a tractor-looking vehicle that identified IEDs with ground-penetrating radar. There was only one soldier who drove the Husky, and his ability to identify IEDs from a grainy green radar screen only came from experience. He either missed an IED resulting in an IED explosion, or he identified rocks under the soil, which forced everyone else to wait in the trucks for the discovery of a rock. Add this pattern up thirty times over an eight-hour patrol and you can understand the level of scrutiny applied to the poor huskey driver. When the huskey identified a suspected IED, he called up the buffalo. The Buffalo was a rectangular armored vehicle with a long excavating arm. The Buffalo's job was digging up the suspected IED with the excavating arm. The Buffalo operator was also trained mostly by experience. If he blew up the IED and damaged the excavating arm, then the patrol lost its RCP capability. Often this meant the patrol returned to the base as a failed mission. If the Husky accurately identified an IED and the Buffalo effectively dug up the IED, then EOD—the third vehicle in the patrol—sent out the robot and rendered the IED safe. As ineffective as the process sounds, the team had perfected the procedure by the time I arrived. It was amazing to watch them work.

The third element I met after arriving at Orgun was the infantry battalion staff from 1-187. The first time the battalion commander met me, he said, "So you're my CIED team leader. I'm not sure what that is. What do you provide me?"

Keep in mind, I only had three days of training in a Hilton lobby. All my other experiences were as a Marine infantry officer. "Shit, sir, I'm not really sure. But I can promise you this, I'm going to integrate into your staff seamlessly, I'm going to make myself smart on the threats, and I'm going to provide value to the team."

"I like you. See you at the 19:00 commander's update brief."

After those initial introductions, I was off to the races. The battalion staff made me feel like a member of the team, and I did everything in my power to hold up my end of the bargain. The secret to any job is developing relationships, making yourself smart, and demonstrating you're a critical player on the team. I spoke with any person on the base who had insight or experience with IEDs, which not only included EOD and RCP, but also the CIA, special forces elements, law enforcement professionals, and young infantry soldiers. In a short amount of time, I was briefing in all the meetings and providing value from a CIED perspective to inform the battalion commander's decision-making process.

I supported the battalion commander for 1-187, but my real boss, the one who wrote my evaluation report, was stationed hours away from my FOB. One of the best things about my Afghanistan deployment was that I never had a field grade officer standing over my shoulder telling me what I should be doing. I truly had the freedom to do what I thought was most effective with my time. I was in the sweet spot as a young captain: still young enough to get outside the wire on a regular basis, but old enough to see the bigger picture. I freely built my schedule based on my interpretation of the requirements. My job only required positive performance feedback from the unit I supported and occasional situation reports directly from me to my boss. Other than that, my value came from understanding the threat so that I could solve problems. And as any young motivated officer can attest, situational awareness is best built experiencing the fight.

The battalion area of operations for 1-187 was widespread. All their company FOBs were at least a day's drive away. One of the company FOBs was named FOB Tillman after the heroic American, Pat Tillman, who left the NFL to serve his country. Tillman died in the area where the FOB was later constructed. The majority of the battalion AO was in the mountains. Typically people think of Afghanistan as desert wasteland, but where I was it felt more like the Colorado Rockies. Every time we dismounted the trucks or conducted a dismounted patrol, the altitude was physically draining.

I remember one mission that paints an accurate picture of the breakdowns in Afghanistan on all levels of war. It was a seemingly simple resupply mission that we planned for a couple of days. The late-summer weather had been very rainy, so it prevented normal air resupplies from getting to the company FOBs. Thus, the battalion organized a larger-than-normal ground resupply mission to one of their company positions. The mission required RCP and EOD to lead the way, so naturally I involved myself in the mission.

The initial patrol went without incident. We found a couple of IEDs, and the dismounted security got into a few firefights to brush the enemy back, but nothing noteworthy. When we arrived at the company FOB, we downloaded all the logistics and then spoke to the company commander. He asked us for an unexpected favor. He asked if we could drive logistics out to one of his platoon positions that also hadn't been resupplied in a while. He felt more comfortable delivering the logistics with the EOD and RCP assets. We called back to the battalion and relayed the request. The battalion approved the additional mission, and so we rearmed/reset and prepared to deliver another round of logistics from the company FOB to the platoon outpost.

For context, this mounted patrol was unnecessarily large. It involved RCP, EOD, infantry from the company, logistical trucks, and the Afghan National Security Forces. When you stood back and looked at the patrol, there were over thirty vehicles of all different types pulled together to deliver logistics to a platoon outpost of only about forty soldiers. The excess of the mission made it hard not to scratch your head.

We departed on the mission around 08:00. We travelled through the creek beds of the mountains the entire mission. There were no roads in this part of the world. We finally pulled out of a creek bed and arrived at the platoon outpost around 14:00 that day. Pulling up to the position, it was clear the position was small and isolated. If or when this position was attacked, there wasn't another ground unit that could save them. Because the outpost had a cliff face on the backside, the platoon commander decided to always keep a squad on the top of the cliff. Thus, he was relegated to a squad on post, a squad living on the cliff face, and a squad on rest and/or ready to patrol. There wasn't a lot of time off at this position.

I took the opportunity as the trucks started off-loading all the logistics to walk around the platoon position. As an executive officer who surveyed platoon positions in Ramadi, I had developed a skill at seeing what the platoon leadership didn't want you to see. It was clear all the soldiers at the position had the thousand-mile stare and needed sleep. None of them wore blouses, and all their T-shirts were disgusting. The gym was made of dirt, ammo cans, and tires. I could tell they had all shaved for our arrival, because they still had tan lines from where their beards had previously protected against the sun. This implied standard slipped when leaders left, but soldiers of the platoon were cognizant enough to put on a fake front when visitors arrived. I concluded that the soldiers on this base didn't come from the same planet as the creatures on Bagram who kept their weapons in trash bags. These were the warriors from my planet. I loved everything about them.

After a tour of the position from the platoon commander, I walked up to one of the security posts and asked the young soldier to tell me about his post. He stood up and pointed to a clear ridgeline about a kilometer away from the position. "That's Pakistan, sir," he said as he pointed. "See the black spot two fingers from the big bush? That's the mortar-firing positions the Taliban uses to shoot at us. It's super frustrating sir, because we aren't allowed to shoot back across the border." I wanted to tell him that he always had the right to self-defense, but the situation was complicated. Self-defense typically relates to a personal firearm. The mortar-firing position was outside his rifle's effective range. He could range it with machine guns, rockets, or mortars, but at that distance it was harder to claim self-defense. Plus, despite the self-defense angle, if it created an international incident, it probably wouldn't end well for the young enlisted soldier. So I said nothing. I fist-bumped the young soldier and walked back to my truck.

I sat in my truck still waiting on the logistical download and contemplated the obvious problems with this platoon's position. The position was created on a main infiltration line used by the Taliban crossing into Afghanistan from Pakistan. But American politicians weren't willing to enter Pakistan to wage war against our enemies. When the attacks of 9/11 happened, President George W. Bush stated that America would make no distinction between the terrorists and the countries that harbored terrorists. Yet even the dirty Army specialist on post there understood the Taliban's home base was western Pakistan. I knew from my CIED research that Miramshaw, Pakistan, which was right across the border, translated to "city of matches." Miramshaw was known for the large match factory in the center of town. Potassium chlorate is the main resource used to make matches. In my AO at that time, all we had were homemade IEDs utilizing potassium chlorate as the explosive. My entire purpose as a CIED team leader was "getting left of the boom." In other words, through analytics and action, disrupting supply routes to prevent IEDs from ever getting emplaced in the AO. But it was infuriating, because we knew exactly where the IEDs were coming from, but we weren't willing to do anything about it.

The more time I spent in Afghanistan, the more I was struck by organization of the Taliban. They were clearly a conventional force. They lacked American's version of morals. But American's just war theory has always been fundamentally flawed. You don't need to be just to win a war. You just need conviction to do what it takes to win. While American and Taliban theories of justice were different, our wartime methods were very similar. The Americans used Kuwaiti bases to facilitate logistics; the Taliban used western Pakistan. It was funny to think about a Muslim man my age flying into the Peshawar, Pakistan, airport, with the same ambiguous guidance as I had received, ultimately being shuffled into the same part of Paktika, Afghanistan, as I had been.

I never received clarity during my entire deployment whether our government considered the Taliban a terrorist threat. I thought it was relevant since I was deployed under the banner of the global war on terrorism. By definition a terrorist is a non-state actor. Did we make the Taliban terrorists when we drove them out of Afghanistan? I understood the need to have a military response on al-Qaeda, a true terrorist organization per the definition, but what were we doing at this point? If the purpose of the mission in Afghanistan was evolving, was this platoon's mission tied to the new operational and strategic goals?

The platoon outpost position was a product of a local battalion commander trying to limit the Taliban's freedom of movement at a level of aggression not congruent with the operational design of the current wartime plans. For a historical example, there were many parallels from the American War in Afghanistan to the German War in World War I. The Germans went into World War I using the Schlieffen plan. The Schlieffen plan was a German war design addressing fighting war against the French and Russians on a two front war simultaneously. There were many reasons the plan failed. I concluded something seemingly obvious yet not often discussed: Germany lost as soon as they executed a plan fighting a war on two fronts. If the German politicians had any sense, they would have secured Russia or France as an ally, and if unable, taken measures to prevent battle at all costs. What nation would be stupid enough to build a plan requiring a two-front war? World War I was completely preventable by the Germans. It was always painful listening to military academics describe something as simple as the Schlieffen plan's failures. Military academics always started the problem assuming the geo-political conditions were unavoidable. We never discussed how generals should better advise politicians on diplomatic/wartime initial plans. Instead, the tactical military problem clouded our ability to identify the seam between politics and military where all wars are won or lost. The academics offered a myriad of marginally interesting but mostly irrelevant details for Germany's failures: "The plan failed because of modified plans... what about train capability... or how about Belgium... don't forget about Russia's response time." It often appeared that academics' heightened education prevented clarity of thought. As soon as I understood the German's initial plan was a two front war, I had a hard time paying attention to the details.

But there was another obscure reason the Schlieffen plan failed. I independently studied the opening gambit of World War I through a series of YouTube videos. Everyone knows in a game of chess, much of the game is largely decided in the opening. The Germans attempted to quickly defeat the French before turning their attention to the Russians. Striking first, the Germans quickly enveloped the French, but German General Kluck penetrated faster and beyond his adjacent units. The German military leadership, worried about a disheveled front, ordered a retreat to regain order of their line. The lost tempo and retreat by the Germans ultimately resulted in stagnation, trench warfare, and played a role in the disintegration of the Schlieffen plan. Shortly after the stagnation in France, the Germans spread their forces thousands of miles apart addressing Russian troops on the eastern front. The war was lost from the very beginning. Comparatively, the Americans failed the opening gambit of their Afghanistan war for similar reasons. They had an opportunity to kill Osama bin Laden early in the war with Task Force 58. But they failed enveloping the Tora Bora region due to the same misplaced restraint. General Mattis commanded Task Force 58 during the missed opportunity. But the restraint emplaced on Task Force 58 came from Rumsfeld's misguided affection for special forces. Following the failed opening gambit in Afghanistan, the Americans then started a war on a second front in Iraq.

The two front approach had obvious problems. But the Americans, Germans, and military academics across the globe failed at grasping the balance between centralized and decentralized control at the appropriate moments in warfare. It appeared political/ military balance seemed out of reach in the modern nation-state warfare model. Consequently, unsuccessful opening war gambits forced operational design changes mid-war. The operational design of the German Army in World War I morphed into a plan of attrition against the French. But the battle of Verdun historically exemplified how changing operational plans don't always account for pre-existing thinking styles of mid-level military commanders. At Verdun, German commanders from the battalion level and up sought battle with one goal in mind: kill the enemy. The German soldier's aggressive behavior was an effective tool when the war time strategy required quick tempo. But it worked against the Germans when the new approach required restraint. Perhaps similarities are not surprising since the American military had such a love fascination with studying the German military. It always bothered me that Americans fixated on a military who hadn't won a war in centuries. The Germans consistently lost wars because they couldn't link tactical aggression with operational design. How could our leaders not see the parallel? Was the same thing happening in Afghanistan? Did our operational plan morph into something requiring a war of attrition? If so, was this platoon position on the border of Pakistan overly aggressive in the same manner as the Germans at Verdun? Should we be exercising more restraint? And where the fuck were the American Generals for that matter? Had any of them ever stepped foot in this platoon outpost. And if they had, why didn't they ask the same questions?

Suddenly I was ripped from my thoughts when the EOD team jumped back in the truck. The team leader informed me the resupply was complete. We left the platoon outpost around 15:00 that day. When we left the weather was sunny, but around 20:00 it got dark, it started raining, and the situation quickly got complicated. While driving down the creek bed, we suddenly found ourselves in a flash flood that can only be described as if someone broke a dam. In an instant the creek bed filled up with water, and the trucks became stuck.

While we processed the situation of the flash flood, we heard over the radio that the Taliban were watching us. To understand the context, on a previous patrol we had inherited Taliban communication devices known as ICOMs from Taliban fighters we killed. We always kept an ICOM in the patrol on scan. When the Taliban communicated, our ICOM picked up the communication. We then had interpreters translate their communication, and we passed that information over our internal radios. As soon as our trucks got stuck in the water, our ICOMs picked up the Taliban chatter, which meant we all knew there was a good chance a firefight was about to ensue. I listened over the vehicle communication devices as the patrol leader called higher headquarters requesting air support for the Taliban threat. The air support was denied because it was raining and it was deemed unsafe.

I was in the third vehicle, the EOD truck, in our massive patrol. I could only see a few of the vehicles in front and back of me through the twisting creek bed. As I evaluated the threats between the water and the Taliban, in the next instant, as if a second dam had broken, the water immediately rose to the base of the windshields. We all were immediately forced to move through the turret holes and stand on the tops of our vehicles. The internal communication devices in the trucks were now inoperable, and we were only left with the handheld radios on our chests. The machine guns in the turrets were still usable and made abandoning the vehicles a tough choice.

It was a dilemma: jump into a ripping river and try to swim to shore with whatever gear you could swim with or stand on top of the truck with the machine gun and hope the water subsided before the enemy ambush began. I made the decision that someone needed to jump in the river and do something. Since I was in the EOD truck and we happened to have plenty of rope, I grabbed as much rope as I could, dropped the rest of my gear, and jumped into the river. The current was ripping, but I was a strong swimmer and made it to the other side. I tied one end of the rope up to a tree and tied the other end to a rock. Then I threw the rock from the shore to the vehicle in the middle of the river. I needed them to catch it so they could tie off their end on the vehicle. I'd like to say I made the throw on one attempt, but it wasn't as easy as in the movies. Despite our terrible situation, the soldiers all laughed at me as I missed the throw multiple times and then pulled the rock back to the shore to try again.

I finally made the throw. Once the rope was tied off on both ends, we had a rope bridge, and were able to safely move the rest of the crew from the vehicle to the shore. I took the rest of the rope and started passing it out down the line of trucks. My rock throwing got better. Other vehicles that had rope started employing the same tactic. Soon everyone began making rope bridges. Those of us on shore immediately set out to help other trucks with their bridges. Once we got enough people ashore, we established perimeter security as best as we could, anticipating the imminent ambush.

Just as it felt we were getting control of the situation, we lost control. One of the American soldiers moving across a rope bridge toward the back of the patrol panicked on the rope when his lower body hit the ripping current. In his panic he let go of the rope and washed away down river. The Afghan National Security Forces in the back of the patrol stated they watched him float past but were unable to save him. Ten minutes later we intercepted communications from the Taliban that they had captured the missing soldier.

The code word for a missing service member was DUSTWUN. When we passed this code over the radio, the previously denied air support was approved. Within twenty minutes a section of Apache helicopters was on station. The section lead was a female. I'll never forget her voice. She saved all our lives that night. When she got on station, we gave her the check-in brief describing the imminent Taliban ambush, and the enemy's probably location. Then we set her free to work. She immediately began scanning the mountainside adjacent to our creek bed.

"I have positive identification of five enemy fighters with what appears to be an RPG. Clear to engage?"

"Cleared hot. Approved."

"I've killed five fighters. There was a secondary explosion. I think it was his RPG. They're all dead. Continuing to scan."

She continued to scan and found three more groups of fighters that night. She must have killed at least twenty people while we sat on the other side of the embankment watching the show as if it was the Fourth of July. I took turns watching her kill people with my NVGs (night vision goggles) on and with my NVGs off. I wanted to experience it from different perspectives. I was most impressed that she never conveyed an emotion over the radio. It was clear this was not her first shooting spree in Afghanistan. She was a pro.

We ended up finding the American soldier the next morning. He had drowned and was never captured by the Taliban. The Taliban, knowing that we listened to their ICOM chatter, passed misinformation over the radio to make us believe the Taliban had captured our man. I don't know whether the Taliban listened to the Afghan National Security Forces radios or someone in the Afghan National Security Force had called and told them what was happening. But either way, their decision to pass misinformation ultimately triggered the Apaches, which led to their death. War is a chaotic place.

The missing solider was located slightly protruding from a stick in the middle of the river. When we found him, his body was contorted in such a way that we believed he might be rigged with explosives. We still didn't know at that time whether the Taliban had possessed him. We couldn't get the robot to scan since he was in the middle of water. But the current and water level had significantly subsided, so my EOD tech felt comfortable enough walking through the river in his bomb suit to check the body. When he deemed it safe, he cut the body off the stick, and it floated down river where I was standing. I caught the body and dragged it out of the river. The first thing I noticed about the dead soldier was his bloated and veiny stomach. The second thing I noticed was his face. He couldn't have been more than twenty.

The resupply mission that resulted in the drowning of a Soldier is a patrol I'll never forget. I quickly realized every patrol in Afghanistan had its own complexities, sacrifices, and unique circumstances. For example, I was on a combat patrol in Afghanistan the December night my first son was born. I anticipated the birth, so I armed one of my friends at the FOB with my family's contact information prior to the patrol. When I returned, my friend was waiting for me with a satellite phone. "You need to call your wife. You're a father now." I called the hospital and was lucky enough to get through to my wife. The nurses seemed to know I was in Afghanistan and went out of their way to connect the call. When I finally connected with her, she had already completed the delivery, and the baby was out of the room getting evaluated. She was still on drugs, but it was nice to hear her voice. All I needed to hear was that she and the baby were healthy, which she assured me was the case.

Service members received two weeks of leave if their deployments were a year or longer. I took mine shortly after my son was born. When I finally got stateside to see my wife, she had already been released from the hospital. We still owned our house in North Carolina, but she decided to have our child in Virginia Beach so her family could serve as a support network. As a result, I found myself travelling to my in-laws to spend my time stateside. If I could have picked one hundred locations to spend during my only two weeks away from combat, my in-laws' house would not be on that list. But I didn't feel entitled to have an opinion. I wasn't there, and so my wife had the right to make decisions that were best for her. I think subconsciously it bothered me that my mother-in-law took care of my son and wife while I was away.

It's powerful meeting your child for the first time after six months of combat. It almost seems surreal. While holding my child for the first time in my in-laws' living room, I was filled with love and connection. After holding him for a while, I eventually passed him back to my mother-in-law, grabbed a beer, and sat on the couch filled with fear and isolation. When I was in combat, I was present in the moment, but when I returned from my patrols, all I could think about was getting back to my family. When I held my son, I was present in the moment, but when I sat on the couch, all I could think about was the six months of combat I still had in front of me. Funny how the mind works. I was grateful to have the opportunity to meet my son in the middle of my deployment, but before I knew it, I returned to Afghanistan.

I could continue to tell war stories about Afghanistan for an entire book. I was in combat for 365 days. On some of those days I did multiple missions that each had their own unique story. But that's not the purpose of this book. Maybe someday I'll write a longer book just about Afghanistan. For now, here is a quick highlight reel:

- Getting into a firefight in a poppy field, touching my eye, having my eye swell shut, and continuing to shoot with my left eye.

- Using a B52 bomber as a flyover in a firefight even though they didn't have any bombs because they were the only external asset available. Admiring the deafening machine. Going back to shooting two minutes later as if it was an intermission.

- Failing to call close air support correctly. Getting our partnered Afghan soldier killed due to our own failures to initiate the attack. Requesting a helicopter to pick up the dead Afghan soldier. Getting denied because the Afghan soldier wasn't American. Carrying the dead body for five miles in complete disgrace.

- Trying to execute multiple raids after a loud UAS flew over the objective, alarming the people we were after. Identifying this as a problem. Having it happen the next five missions.

- Realizing burning shit was bad. Learning to shit into a wag bag. Realizing on long vehicle patrols that females needed a funnel to piss into bottles like the rest of us.

- Trying to pull intelligence off dead bodies. Realizing movies never show how rigor mortis makes it impossible to manipulate a dead person.

- Responding to an IED explosion with five passengers. Evacuating four unconscious passengers and not the conscious passenger. Watching the conscious passenger die in front of us from internal injuries we were too stupid to triage.

- Killing my first person with a rifle.

- Watching a cornered Taliban member fight to the death and in his last breath pull pin on a grenade and lie on it. Experiencing a moment where I felt like he was braver than me.

- Sitting in the EOD truck when our machine gunner was hit with an RPG and fell into the truck. Jumping on the gun and pretending like my injured teammate wasn't there.

- Watching a six-year-old boy throw a grenade at our mounted patrol and the turret gunner swing his machine gun toward the boy. Watching the boy walk away as the machine gunner chose not to shoot.

- Sending a blimp up with cameras from our FOB so that we could see for miles. Realizing that the blimp also provided a target for the enemy to shoot at us from miles.

- Receiving indirect fire every day. Becoming numb to the indirect fire after a couple of months. Playing spades while rounds exploded around us.

- Getting an Army Commendation for Valor and a Bronze Star for dynamic missions.

- Stepping on an IED and not having it explode.

- Being shot at by the Taliban while the Polish supported us on the mission. Calling the Polish and requesting fire support assistance. Having the Polish tell me they couldn't help because their national laws required them to be shot at directly.

- Being kicked out of the chow hall before it closed because I had on combat gear and not clean FOB clothes.

- Being left on a mountain. Realizing I was going to freeze to death on the mountain. Sleeping in a body bag spooning another man to prevent from freezing on a mountain.

The list goes on and on, but again, is not the point of this book. However, there is one other story worth sharing to illustrate my Afghanistan experience. Just before I returned home for my leave, I received word that First Lieutenant Robert Kelly, the Marine from 1/8 who I spent a lot of time with, was leading a patrol in RC SW, stepped on an IED, and was killed instantly. It was hard for me to stomach the news. I had tried to convince Kelly not to become an officer on one hand, and on the other hand, I had written him a recommendation to become an officer. I looked up to him in many ways even though I outranked him. I remembered through his own words how much he loved the Marines and America. Because of the loss, it was hard not to question his sacrifice and decisions.

Six months later, in April 2011, the Secretary of Defense, Robert Gates, assigned Lieutenant General Kelly as his deputy. Robert Gates at that time was about to step down as the secretary of defense and went on a tour in Afghanistan to see all the troops in the combat zone before he departed. At this time, I had moved locations and was at a place called FOB Andar in the Ghazni Province. Robert Gates looked at the significant events tracker to pick the worst battalion headquarter FOBs to visit, and sure enough, FOB Andar was at the top of the list. We received indirect fire every day. Anticipating their visit, the 101st flooded the battlespace with a battalion of infantry to ensure the Taliban would have a difficult time shooting at us.

Secretary of Defense Gates and General Kelly both arrived and toured the FOB. They were able to experience the only time the FOB wasn't shot at with indirect fire. At a certain point, General Kelly realized a single Marine resided on the desolate base of Army soldiers and walked up to me to start a conversation. He asked me about my job and the deployment. When it felt appropriate in the conversation, I informed him that we had met five years before at A.P. Hill. I reminded him that I was the second lieutenant his son had introduced him to. He acted like he remembered me, but I'm sure he didn't. Then I was brave enough to tell him how highly I thought of his son, that in my opinion, his son represented everything we fought for. General Kelly took the compliment and then changed the conversation. The pain he was suffering was still too raw. When the conversation was over, General Kelly and Secretary of Defense Gates left, and I never spoke to General Kelly again.

My time in Afghanistan profoundly impacted me in many ways. It changed me as a man. It was so emotionally and physically draining that I knew I needed time on the backside of the deployment to stabilize. I couldn't get out of the Marine Corps as soon the deployment ended and be what my family needed me to be. As I struggled with what to do next, I was selected by the Marine Corps to attend a formal school called Expeditionary Warfare School (EWS). It was a one-year resident school in Quantico, Virginia, designed to prepare officers to work on a staff. I talked to my wife about it, and we decided to accept the orders to the school. I knew by accepting the orders that there was a two-year requirement of obligated service on the backside of the school. But the reset time after the deployment was all I could think about. In July 2011, I made my way out of Afghanistan and back to Quantico.

CHAPTER 7:

WHAT IF LEADERS HAVE THE WRONG FOCUS? — EXPEDITIONARY WARFARE SCHOOL. REAWAKENING. COMPANY COMMAND.

"Those who aren't living up to the title Marine within our midst are disrupting the return to immediate readiness, soiling our honor, and causing the American people to lose trust in us! Disregarding orders and standards, substance abuse, sexual assault, self-destructive behavior, and failure to maintain personal fitness and appearance standards, weakens our Corps and dishonors all who have endured wars' hardships. This insurgency of wrongdoing is invading our homes and destroying our credibility."

—Marine Corps Commandant Amos

October 2013 white letter to the force explaining why the military was losing credibility during failed wars: NCOs not Generals.

When I returned from deployment, I spent one night in Washington, DC, collecting my orders and completing my out-processing with JIEDDO. The following day I met my wife at a hotel south of Quantico. After leaving the hotel, we found out later she was pregnant with my second son. I had left for Afghanistan in my twenties with no children, and shortly after returning from Afghanistan I was in my thirties with two sons. Life was changing.

While at EWS, in addition to learning how to become a father, I was also dealing with the psychological and physical changes in my body following a year of combat. My anxiety returned full force. I returned to the emergency room a couple of times only to receive the same clean bill of health as I did post-Ramadi. But now, in addition to the chest pains, I was also dealing with vision blurriness and face numbness. It got to the point that I needed additional help. Luckily, my instructor was understanding and allowed me time away from class to speak to different naval medicine psychologists and doctors. This path was long and is not the purpose of the book. But suffice it to say, I eventually got my anxiety under control. The moral of the story is that combat does not damage service members. It makes them stronger. Posttraumatic growth. However, that doesn't mean veterans don't need treatment from time to time. But I never allowed my postdeployment issues to define me as a victim. I chose to go to combat. I loved every second of it. Once I was able to get treatment, I only came out on the other side stronger.

There are a few random stories from my time at EWS that are relevant to the larger themes. First, my director of EWS at the time was a man named Colonel David Close. There was one thing I remembered him saying all the time. "If you're not happy being a Marine, then you need to get out." He made this statement all the time. I was always troubled by it. He made the service member's choice of getting out of the military seem so binary. There were many days I wasn't happy serving in the Marine Corps. But

Marines, to include the battalion commander, were not allowed to transfer out of the unit until the investigation was finally concluded. All except the former commandant's son, the battalion executive officer of 3/2, Major Conway. Major Conway was granted a special exception. He was the only Marine allowed out of the unit. They moved him to Hawaii, where he assumed command within the next six months.

General Amos came to speak to us one other time while I was at EWS. He called the second speaking tour the Heritage Brief. He developed a term called the *reawakening*. Somehow, he determined that the NCO corps was failing in their responsibilities to the organization. Ironic since the NCO corps was winning every tactical battle. It was the general officers who didn't understand how to tie tactical success to policy objectives. General Amos spoke about discipline and what that meant to the success of the Marine Corps. His idea of discipline was placing cameras in the barracks so that leaders could watch the Marines as if they were in prison. His philosophy was completely foreign to the trust we should have in our junior enlisted. It is a philosophy that still permeates the general officers corps.

I didn't know it at the time, but following EWS I would eventually end up assigned to 3/2, the same unit involved in the Taliban urination incident. It was unclear at the time because I initially received orders to the unit 2/2. I was assigned with one other officer named Andrew Nicholson. Captain Nicholson was the son of the famous Lieutenant General Lawrence D. Nicholson. General Nicholson had commanded RC SW in Afghanistan. In other words, he commanded the Marine Forces in Afghanistan. Everyone knew who he was. Thus, my peer had name recognition that I did not. When it came time to execute orders, I was told I would be temporarily assigned to Officer Candidate School for the summer to help augment before checking into 2/2. Captain Nicholson was absolved of this additional temporary responsibility. He checked into 2/2 immediately and assumed command of his company while I stayed in Quantico.

When I checked into Officer Candidate School as a summer augment, I was given the choice of teaching in an academics section or serving as a platoon commander. The academics job would have been much less taxing, but I was a leader. If I was there, I was going to lead. I asked to be a platoon commander. Thus, for three months I served as a platoon commander at Officer Candidate School. Platoon commanders at Officer Candidate School lead every physical event. It was a physically and spiritually draining three-month tour. I was drinking Monsters in my canteens to stay awake.

While I was at OCS, the 2/2 battalion commander Lieutenant Colonel Steven Wolf came up and had lunch with me. He told me I was going to assume command of Echo Company when I eventually checked into 2/2. But after he left, I received indications that 3/2, a unit in the same regiment, had aggregated to the MEU short a Headquarters and Service Company commander. This implied there was a high probability that when I checked into 2d Marines, I would be pushed to 3/2 instead of 2/2. I emailed Lieutenant Colonel Wolf and told him what I had heard. I said, "Sir, I'm hearing that when I check into 2d Marines they may push me out of 2/2 and into 3/2 to become the Headquarters Company Commander. You promised me Echo Company. I'd prefer not to be a Headquarters Company Commander. Should I reach out to the monitor and try to avoid 2d Marines? Or is there any way I can compete with Captain Nicholson who checked in to your unit before me because I was sent to augment OCS?"

He emailed me back (I still have the email): "Stu, your reputation precedes you. I was very impressed by you when we spoke. I know you are a great officer. You will be a rifle company commander in my battalion. If I can't make you a rifle company commander in my battalion, I will ensure you are a rifle company commander in another battalion. You will not be a Headquarters Company Commander."

His response suppressed my fears about being pushed to 3/2. I eventually checked into 2/2 in September 2012. Lieutenant Colonel Wolf was on leave when I checked in. As soon as I checked in, 2d Marines changed my orders and pushed me to 3/2 exactly as I had predicted. The regimental commander at the time was a man named Colonel Bill Jurney. Since Lieutenant Colonel Wolf was on leave, I sought out Colonel Jurney while he was on the Camp Lejeune parade field rehearsing a division change of command. I was brave enough to walk up to him and introduce myself. I explained my situation and asked him if there was any way to compete with Captain Nicholson for a Rifle Company or transfer to another unit for a Rifle Company as Lieutenant Colonel Wolf had promised.

He looked at me with contempt. "New captains don't rate shit. You will go where you are told. But because you were brave enough, or stupid enough, to come up and speak to me, I will listen to what Lieutenant Colonel Wolf has to say."

I left the parade field and checked into 3/2 as the headquarters company commander that afternoon. When Lieutenant Colonel Wolf returned from his leave, he did email me and admit he made the decision to send me to 3/2. He didn't address why it was the opposite of what he told me earlier or why I didn't get to compete with the general's son, but his tone in the email acknowledged my frustration. He said I could come speak to him if I was upset about it. But I calculated that whining about my perceived mistreatment after the decision was made wasn't beneficial to my situation. I never spoke to Lieutenant Colonel Wolf again, and I prepared myself to be the best Headquarters and Service Company commander possible in my new unit 3/2.

Immediately after assuming 3/2 Headquarters Company, we prepared for our deployment on the 26th Marine Expeditionary Unit. As we began our workup, the event in Benghazi, Libya, took place. President Obama, Vice President Biden, and Secretary of State Clinton watched on TV screens as Americans fought enemies 1 vs. 1000. The Africom Combatant commander at the time, General Carter Ham, had plenty of military options available to respond to the incident. But he was allegedly told by the political leaders to stand down and let Americans die. And General Ham did exactly what General McKenzie stated later that he had done: "Followed orders." America's general officers have lost the ability to make morally courageous decisions. General Ham never received the scrutiny he deserved. He continued to command and went on to a comfortable retirement without scruple.

The Benghazi incident directly impacted me in more ways than obvious disappointment with my senior leaders. The incident forced a MEU to park off the coast of Libya. As a result, my upcoming deployment was needed sooner and for longer duration as the global reserve. My upcoming deployment on the 26th MEU was extended to ten months. It was as long as they could make it without giving us a two-week break during the deployment.

I deployed on the 26th MEU from March 2013 to December 2013. During the deployment we mostly conducted bilateral engagements with foreign militaries in places like Egypt, Jordan, Oman, Qatar, Djibouti, and Europe. We never engaged in combat on that deployment. During this time, General Amos, the commandant, continued pushing the new direction of the Marine Corps and the reawakening. The narrative of the Marine Corps changed again. When once I was made to feel ignorant because I hadn't been to Iraq, and then again because I hadn't been to Afghanistan, now those experiences worked against me. The new narrative was, "It's not important than you've been to Iraq and Afghanistan. If you weren't around pre 9/11, then you're a product of the wartime generation, which means you don't know how to effectively train a unit." Even though this line of thinking was insulting and bothersome, my battalion commander forced all the company commanders to facilitate teaching this new information. We taught multiple classes to the Marines across the battalion. We all needed to reiterate our battalion commander's interpretation of the commandant's intent, which was "if you didn't agree with the new direction of the Marine Corps you needed to get out." I realized as I taught the classes how frustrated I was becoming. It seemed like no matter what I accomplished in the Marine Corps, there was always someone telling me that "I didn't understand because I hadn't experienced X." At what point does a new-generation Marine become an old-generation Marine?

Even though I was initially disappointed to be assigned as the Headquarters and Service Company commander, I lived the cliché, "bloom where you are planted." I did everything I could to be the commander all my Marines needed. Not only did I command all the supporting elements in the battalion, but I also had an engineer and reconnaissance platoon. It's hard to distinguish yourself as the Headquarters Company commander when competing against rifle company commander peers whose purpose is more in line with the purpose of the battalion. But by end of the deployment, I demonstrated my abilities as a leader with my battalion commander, and he rewarded me with the top company commander evaluation. Perhaps it was insecurity, but at that point, the validation in terms of the report meant more than it probably should have.

My battalion commander also told me as we returned from the deployment that he selected me as the operations officer for the battalion's follow-on deployment. In terms of experience, at that time, I had been a captain for over five years but was still not yet selected for major. An operations officer is typically a major or at a minimum a captain selected to major. Since I was neither of these, the regiment denied the request. Thus, my battalion commander sat me down and explained he needed to assign a captain who was selected to major. It always put me off that the military placed people in positions based strictly on time rather than performance. The best people should be assigned to billets over the typical career-progression model. But that's not how it worked. Once my battalion commander explained this to me, it put me in an awkward position. I had a decision to make. I could have left the battalion since I had completed my required company command tour. But in the Marine Corps infantry community, Headquarters and Service Company is a place where less talented officers can be hidden. I didn't want my peers assuming I was below average. It wasn't as if I could walk around with my performance evaluation as validation. I understood the critical nature of reputation and perception in the Marine Corps. So, after a year and a half as a company commander, I agreed to stay in the battalion and assume the Weapons Company Command for another year and a half.

Weapons Company Command in 3/2 had its own challenges. Not only did I still have the remnants of the sniper platoon from the 3/2 urination incident, but during that deployment I also inherited most of the mortar Marines from the 1/9 mortar explosion at Hawthorne, where a training incident killed seven Marines instantly and severely wounded many more. The battalion commander and company commander were relieved. No officers above the lieutenant colonel level were held accountable, as is usually the case. Shortly after that incident, the unit 1/9 was disbanded. The Marines with enough time for another deployment were pushed to 3/2, and most of the mortar Marines were then pushed to my company. In 2014, 3/2 Weapons Company had all the misplaced children of the fatalistic events in the Marine Corps.

As I assumed command of Weapons Company, a new battalion commander checked into 3/2. His name was Lieutenant Colonel Timothy Powledge. Lieutenant Colonel Powledge was truly a warrior of our generation. He was a company commander during two very kinetic Iraq deployments. The man had lost Marines in command multiple times, to include his company executive officer. I admired him not only for his combat experience, but also because of his intelligence. Lieutenant Colonel Powledge was a School of Advanced Warfighting (SAW) planner. For context, after the failures of Vietnam, the military developed an advanced operational planning school in each of the services. The thought process was an advanced planning credential would produce staff officers capable of building plans with critical thought. Seeking accreditation and recognition for the course, the military then mistakenly filled these schools with Ivy League educated PhD instructors lacking real combat experience. The military leaders who created the advanced planning credential didn't anticipate how the process would do more to mass produce group think for influential decision makers than any other establishment in the military.

Lieutenant Colonel Powledge probably had the most influence on me in terms of leadership after Lieutenant Colonel Hobbs. He was one of the few officers who appeared to truly care about his Marines. But even though he cared about them, he wasn't afraid to push them to excellence. During our work-up for deployment, my wife was pregnant with our third son and due in November 2014. During November 2014 while my wife was very pregnant with our third son, I was in the California Mojave Desert conducting Infantry Training Exercise, the service level exercise for training prior to a deployment. As the Weapons Company commander, I was also the fire support officer for the Battalion. I deconflicted and approved multiple fire missions as the individual rifle companies executed dynamic live-fire ranges. The final exercise was known as the battalion assault course. It was the one event where Lieutenant Colonel Powledge would be evaluated as a battalion commander. The execution of the event was three days before the birth of my third son. Lieutenant Colonel Powledge pulled me aside and told me to fly home and be with my wife. I was floored. I immediately argued with him. We had assistant fire support officers but none with my experience and training. If the battalion lost me, it would be a huge hit to its responsive fire support capability. He needed me probably more than any other officer in the battalion. But he stayed firm in his conviction. "Stu, you already missed the birth of one child. I know the toll all your deployments have had on your family. I'm not asking you. I'm telling you. Go home."

Most officers in that moment would have told me to execute the battalion assault course and then race home to be with my wife. There was a three-day gap where I could have possibly completed both. But Lieutenant Colonel Powledge wasn't even going to allow me to take the chance of missing the birth. His placed my family above his performance. I was able to see the birth of my third son in the hospital outside Camp Lejeune. My battalion commander's selfless service made me dedicated to him for the rest of the deployment.

The unit deployed six weeks after the birth of my third son. About the time my wife was able to get out of the bed and move around, I left her with a baby and my other two young children. The unit deployed to Okinawa, Japan, on what the Marine Corps calls a Unit Deployment Program (UDP). The purpose of the UDP is for the military to advertise a force in readiness for North Korean aggression. But much like my previous deployment with 3/2, all we ended up doing was conducting bilateral training with foreign nations. This time we trained with the Filipinos, Japanese, and South Koreans.

Despite my loyalty to Lieutenant Colonel Powledge, the weight of battalion command slowly started to change him as a leader. He realized a year into his command that risk-averse behavior was the key to success/survival. In his first year of command, he allowed his company commanders freedom to aggressively train. But by the second year of his command, once we were on deployment and he had established himself, he fell back on a prevent defense mentality. He refused to allow my snipers to conduct a sniper screener in the heat of Okinawa. The regimental commander, Colonel David Odom, threatened Lieutenant Colonel Powledge with ramifications if the unit had any heat casualties. At least, that's what Lieutenant Colonel Powledge said. But I knew Colonel Odom had probably only said something like, "Heat casualties are starting to be a problem. Please ensure you pay attention to this." That's how senior officers threaten. The system compels commanders to pull a threat out of a seemingly harmless comment. So Lieutenant Colonel Powledge in turn asked me as the Weapons Company commander to promise I wouldn't have a heat casualty. I stated, "These are all the controls we have in place. We will do everything we can to prevent a heat casualty. We will also have all the controls in place to treat a heat casualty if it occurs. But we can't promise someone won't be a heat casualty." That response wasn't good enough. He refused to allow us to conduct the operation. Additionally, prior to deployment, the battalion had a Marine killed in a recreational ATV accident. In response to that, as we prepared to return from deployment, during a meeting with me and all the other company commanders, Lieutenant Colonel Powledge made it clear that annual training was the priority. When we all started articulating other warfighting training priorities, he went back to the ATV incident. "Do you remember Corporal X who died on the ATV incident? Thank God he had completed the annual training 101 days of summer. Do you know what the general would have done had he not completed the training?" Despite my love for the man, I don't think I ever forgave him for that comment.

Finally, I was promoted to major one month prior to completion of our deployment. The promotion necessitated a grade-change evaluation report. It also meant that my evaluations were now in competition with the other majors in the battalion. Lieutenant Colonel Powledge pulled me in his office and congratulated me on my performance as a captain. He gave me the top report. But then, without offering much other feedback, he told me my report as a major would be the lowest report in his profile on my way out the door. He stated, "Look, the operations officer has been outperforming the executive officer, and I need a young major to boost my profile so that the executive officer has a chance to get battalion command. I need you to be a team player."

At the time I kept my mouth shut. But as I stewed on his comments, I became frustrated. *Shouldn't an officer be evaluated on their performance and not a pre-destined agreement to ensure everyone is treated fairly*, I thought. My frustration on this matter finally boiled over, and I shot him an email stating, "Sir, you have an option to give me a non-observed evaluation on the way out the door since the evaluation time will be less than 90 days. If you are not willing to do that, I expect you give me a path to compete with the other majors in the battalion. I don't think it's fair that I am predestined to be your lowest report to help out the other majors career progression."

Lieutenant Colonel Powledge pulled me in his office and yelled at me. We ended our time together with an uncomfortable tension. However, ultimately, he gave me a non-observed report as a major on my way out the door. I felt it was his way of neutralizing our tension at the end.

I was very comfortable as the Weapons Company commander in 3/2. I felt my company could have competed with any unit in the Marine Corps at that time. I knew all my Marines, and they all knew me. Ironic that in my later ordeal, none of those Marines, many of whom were still serving in the Marine Corps, were questioned about what they thought of me as a leader. After two years of company command at SOI and three years of company command in 3/2, I understood very well how to command a unit of 150 to 300 Marines. I had mastered training at the company level while balancing the overwhelming needs of the battalion.

Despite my desire to become the battalion operations officer, at that point I had already been in 3/2 for three years. The Marine Corps determined that amount of time was too long in a stable geographic location (even though I spent most of it on deployment) and decided it was time to move my family. We returned from the UDP deployment in the end of August 2015. I received orders to The Basic School. My check-in was in October 2015. My two older children were already in school at this point, and my wife felt it wasn't healthy to disrupt them mid–school year. So, my wife and I made the decision that it was best if I became a "geo-bachelor." Thus, I traveled to Quantico and lived there by myself until the summer of 2016 when my family could seamlessly transition. After spending only two months with my third child, I moved up to Quantico by myself. I spent the next year driving to see my family on the weekends. When my family finally did come up to live with me the following year, one of my sons made the comment, "It's nice to have a dad again. We didn't have a dad the last couple of years."

CHAPTER 8:

I'M A WHITE AMERICAN MALE WITH A GERMAN LAST NAME. AM I EVIL?—THE BASIC SCHOOL. EQUAL OPPORTUNITY. STANDARDS.

"I am not a racist. I am against every form of racism and segregation. Every form of discrimination."

—Malcom X

I reported to The Basic School in October 2012 as a newly promoted major. Upon arrival, I was assigned as the assistant operations officer. The commanding officer at the time was a man named Colonel Christian Wortman. Colonel Wortman epitomized the ideals of a quality officer. He was intelligent, articulate, personable, and relatable. He spent time in the field regularly teaching lieutenants shoulder to shoulder with the rest of the instructor cadre. This wasn't a requirement for his billet, but he understood the importance of emphasizing the main effort at the school: teaching young lieutenants how to be leaders and provisional rifle platoon commanders. The Marines all respected him for it.

Seven months into my tour, the operations officer, a senior lieutenant colonel, received orders and moved out of the command. Following his departure, Colonel Wortman placed his trust in me and assigned me as the operations officer for The Basic School. It was an honor to serve as a regimental operations officer as a brand-new major. I focused on harnessing relationships and ensuring that operations remained on schedule. My nightmare was three hundred lieutenants showing up to a range and sitting around only to discover the range wasn't properly scheduled. Fortunately, we avoided any major disruptions to the training.

I quickly realized as the operations officer at The Basic School that the primary mission of training young lieutenants was not always the focus. I was amazed at how much diversity and female inclusion absorbed the bandwidth of the instructor staff. I spent more time running down statistics for various congressional panels than I did overseeing day-to-day operations of the school's core mission. The Defense Advisory Committee on Women in the Services (DACOWITS) seemed to ask questions on a weekly basis. Whenever these questions were pushed down, it became the top priority for me as the operations officer. Infantry Officer Course fell under The Basic School. DACOWITS's primary concern was females not getting a fair opportunity to compete with males at the infantry officer producing school house. I must have written at least fifteen separate point papers and created over a dozen statistics-filled briefs on the matter. The excessive back and forth prompted Secretary of the Navy Ray Maybus to personally visit The Basic School to address the tension.

Ray Maybus came down and told us that President Obama wanted to ensure the military was representative of the population and that everyone had an opportunity to serve in all career fields. On the surface, no one disagreed with the sentiment. But the nagging problem under the surface was one of standards. The Marines were reluctant to lower the standards in the name of equal opportunity. During the question-and-answer portion of Ray's speech, one of the captains was brave enough to ask, "Sir, can you address standards? Will standards change?"

"Standards won't change. But they will evolve," stated the secretary of the Navy confidently.

After he left, we were more confused than before he arrived. "So are the standards going to change?" I overheard one Marine ask another. "No, sergeant. They will evolve," said the other in a condescending manner. They both started laughing. I pretended not to hear. I didn't want them to ask my opinion.

To further illustrate the complications of equal opportunity in the military, I developed an analogy with the NBA and WNBA. This analogy is overly simplistic and doesn't correlate directly to war. Attributes needed in war are much more complex than basketball. But the analogy raises questions worth addressing. The WNBA is a product of equal opportunity. It is not equality. Equality means every player, regardless of gender, tries out for the same team, and the most talented players are selected. In the military, it became unclear if we wanted equal opportunity or equality. The distinction is critical because the ramifications in war are final. Hypothetically imagine a basketball game played against two teams and the stakes of the game are death. The losing team will die no matter how fair, courageous, or honorable the game is played. One team is the equality team, meaning only the best players are selected. And the other team is the equal opportunity team, meaning an equal number of spots are reserved for diversity. If you were a parent and you were forced to stake your child's life to the outcome of the game, which team would you pick?

I rotated out of the operations officer billet and into a company commander billet at The Basic School in August 2016. While the operations officer job had long but predictable hours, the company commander billet had an unforgiving schedule. And unfortunately, it coincided with when my family moved up to live with me again. Yet, despite the long hours, it was still nice to sleep in the same bed as my wife every night.

Even as a company commander at The Basic School, I found myself spending a disproportionate amount of time discussing equal opportunity. The Marine Corps has a very low proportion of minorities and females in the general officer ranks. This is quantifiably provable. However, the deeper problem, not often discussed, is that most general officers in the Marine Corps are selected from the infantry officer career field. This makes sense since the Marine Corps is built around the infantry. Females weren't getting through the physical standards of infantry officer course, which is why DACOWITS was applying full-court pressure. But minority males were a different story. Black Marine Corps officers statistically did not pursue infantry as a career choice. When asked why, most of them usually stated, "I want a marketable skill." There is a much lower proportion of black officers (relative to the total population of black officers) going into the infantry compared to the proportion of white officers going into the infantry. This is also quantifiably true. So, leaders at The Basic School, facing pressure from political leadership to make more minorities general officers, tried to figure out how to get more minority officers into combat arm specialties. And most specifically, black officers into infantry officer course. As a company commander, I delivered a sales pitch specifically targeting the minority officers in the company. We were directed to tell all the white males they weren't invited to the speech. Then we explained to all the minorities how important it was for minority officers to pursue combat arms in the Marine Corps. When I left the conversation that day, two black lieutenants came up to me after the event and questioned me.

"Sir, we don't think it's fair that you are treating us differently. We think the best way to deal with equality is to treat everyone as equals." I didn't know what to say. I agreed with them, but I couldn't tell them that. I maintained the party line and reiterated how important it was for them to seriously consider a combat arms specialty.

This trend also surfaced during military occupational specialty selection. Other than training lieutenants how to be leaders and warfighters, our next biggest responsibility was assigning occupational specialties to the students. There were normally only three factors that went into the calculation: lineal standing, needs of the Marine Corps, and preference of the lieutenant. However, the fourth whispered factor was equal opportunity. We were ordered to give minorities and females requesting combat arms their preference without scruple. Once that demographic was identified, we could then ascertain how to assign the rest of the white male population based on remaining availability.

Ironically, the infantry officer director at that time was a black officer, Major Evan Bradley. I considered us friends and respected his opinion on the matter more than all the others. He thought the problem was societal and that trying to force minorities into combat arms within the confines of the military system was shortsighted. He felt minority families needed engagement by the military at much younger ages. We never came to a consensus on how best to accomplish that or whether it even was the military's responsibility for such an undertaking. But I thought it was insightful, nonetheless.

Evan had a tough time as the director at infantry officer course. His billet coincided with a time when females first formally attended the course. He was required to give periodic updates on each female's progress through the school's staff to the commandant's office. He was also constantly taking phone calls from the commandant's office with recommended tweaks to the hike progression and combat endurance test all resulting from female attrition. The commandant's office never put anything in emails; it always communicated by phone calls. There were times significant changes were made to training only days before an event. And Evan's captains mostly implemented the changes. Evan was relegated to his office or pulled to DC as a speaker for DACOWITS. He had very little time to focus on infantry training. The political bureaucracy ultimately compelled Evan to leave the director position at the two-year mark despite leadership's pleas to keep him a third year.

The political tension was felt by everyone. The initiatives even permeated the student population. I have one example from my company command at The Basic School illustrating the frustrations and complexities of these issues. As the commander, I developed and led a company-sized physical-style competition. It started with my company of 300 students divided into two groups. Each student paired up with another student and completed push-ups to failure. The half who completed more push-ups than their competitor remained in the competition. The remaining competitors continued pairing up with each other and competing in different physical events until the 300 was whittled down to one winner. Toward the end there were five remaining students. The other 295 students surrounded the final five contestants. As I walked into the center of the circle, I realized one of the finalists was a female lieutenant named Smith. "Smith!" I exclaimed. "Look at you!" I walked up and gave her a fist bump without a second thought. I was proud of her. But as I did, I heard male lieutenants behind me whispering, "Why didn't he give any fist bumps to the male finalists?" In a moment where the female proved she could play on the equality team, it still came with complications. My subconscious reaction to Smith's accomplishment was that she deserved more accolades than the males. It was difficult for me to separate my values from my leadership style. As a man, I was raised to treat women with respect. I was raised to treat women differently than men. I fundamentally believe men and women are different. I gave Smith a fist bump because I was excited to see a female in the finals. But to some of the men, even though it was a rather insignificant gesture, it immediately signaled my bias. This is a complicated issue that I'm not sure has a simple answer.

I enjoyed my time at The Basic School, but I was ready to leave after three years. My final billet at The Basic School was as the warfighting director. The most influential positions at The Basic

School are the commanding officer, operations officer, warfighting director, and infantry officer director. When I checked out, the commanding general of Training Command (my boss's boss), the commanding officer of The Basic School (the first non-infantry CO), the operations officer, and the infantry officer director were all black officers. All of them were very talented. But statistically, there is a much lower number of black officers in the field-grade ranks than white officers. The statistical anomaly of all the leadership positions at The Basic School being filled with a specific demographic made me pause. Either it was a weird coincidence or it was done intentionally.

Two years later, Lieutenant Colonel Hobbs my old boss from School of Infantry who had then been promoted to colonel, retired from the Marine Corps. As soon as he retired, he published an article titled, "The Marine Corps: Always Faithful—To White Men." I will quote the relevant passages:

> The racist outcomes of deeply entrenched policy exists in the Marine Corps. My goal is to illustrate those effects and to introduce a possible solution using the Marine Corps' method for assigning occupational specialties to officers as a vehicle.... The occupational specialty assignment process of Marine officers results in racist outcomes, and it illustrates how racist policy operates under the surface while powerfully reinforcing inequity.... What is in dispute is whether the institution creates a level playing field for all officers. I believe the institution has not and does not. The institution is biased towards middle- and upper-class white culture. The institution perpetuates the unspoken narrative of white superiority by setting up minority officers for failure. It puts minority officers in occupational specialties

they did not want or have not been thorough-
ly prepared for by the system.... Martin Luther
King Jr., in paraphrasing the abolitionist Theo-
dore Parker, said "the arc of the moral universe is
long, but it bends toward justice." Maybe so, but
not without deliberate force. Newton's first law of
motion, the law of inertia, states things in motion
stay in motion unless acted on by a greater force.
King himself was that force in bending our nation
away from Jim Crow and toward civil rights. Perhaps this essay can be the start of introspection
and real discussion on systemic bias within the
Marine Corps.

I emailed and called Colonel Hobbs following the publication
of this article. Even though I was his subordinate, I cared about
him as a person, and I was worried about him. In many ways, this
man had saved my career when the machine gun optics went missing at SOI. I felt I owed him a lot. When we spoke on the phone,
I asked him about his family and wanted to know if there was anything I could do for him. Once, I realized he wasn't going to let me
help, I addressed his content. I asked why he didn't say anything
while wearing the uniform if he felt so strongly that the organization was racist. I felt he marginalized his message by waiting until
he got out. He now appeared complicit and angry after the fact. He
stated that he didn't have the realization until after he exited the
Marine Corps. I then tried to explain everything that was happening at TBS. I told him about the sales pitch we made to minorities
to get them into combat arms. I told him how this was off-putting
to black lieutenants who only wanted to be treated as equals. I told
him how TBS leaderships positions were almost exclusively filled
with black officers.

He said, "Stu we need more diversity. Diversity makes us a
stronger force."

"Is that historically true, sir? Does history demonstrate the most diverse force wins wars, or does history demonstrate that the best trained warfighting force with the strongest will ultimately wins the war? I'm not saying both attributes can't coexist, but should one be prioritized over the other?"

Then he said, "Stu, I love you, but you'll never understand because you're white." That's when the conversation ended. I was hurt following the conversation. How do you have an intelligent conversation with someone about the facts of a situation if you are automatically discredited because of the color of your skin? I never spoke to Colonel Hobbs directly again. But he still had plenty to say about me publicly when I went through my ordeal.

CHAPTER 9:

WHY DO WE ALLOW LEADERS TO TREAT US LIKE THAT?—COMMAND & STAFF. MARSOC. 6TH MARINES.

"Republics decline into democracies and democracies degenerate into despotism."

—Aristotle

Following my tour at The Basic School, I was screened and selected for Command and Staff College at Marine Corps University. I checked into my new assignment in July 2018. This assignment provided some needed time with my family. I finally had the opportunity to drive my children to school every day and attend school functions. It was a well-needed break in pace even though it wasn't a vacation. Command and Staff College required at least eighty pages of reading a night. It also seemed like a writing school more than anything. I found myself bringing my laptop and writing papers at every soccer practice.

I always thought Command and Staff College could be more effective. First, too much importance was placed on academic PhDs with zero military experience. It was hard to take them seriously when they lectured me about my views. The PhDs also acted like tenured instructors only willing to put in the minimum effort. I would hand them papers they didn't have time to review based on length. Second, the instructors expected me as the infantry officer to carry many of the conversations in the small group discussions. The staff literally pulled me out of class multiple times and stated this directly. It often felt like it was my responsibility to bring my non-infantry peers up to my level instead of the staff bringing me to another level. That being said, the strength of the school was undeniably the students. I learned more from my peers than I did my instructors. But I often wished the staff met me at my level of ability and pushed me as an individual rather than prioritizing the small group's aggregate understanding.

While at the school, I decided to pursue my master's degree. It was an additional requirement but attainable with my flexible schedule. I was excited to explore from an academic perspective my frustrations with how America conducted war. There were many ways to approach my frustrations. I first thought about exploring my disdain for counterinsurgency. The topic provided an opportunity to address people like General Mattis and General David J. Petraeus whom the military and American people lionized despite their inability to win war, but I felt that problem resided too much on the tactical level. I concluded that military leaders would still fall short if the national security council couldn't produce a more effective system for implementing strategy. I also thought about addressing the fallacy of just war theory and how history doesn't demonstrate that the morally superior army wins wars. History demonstrates that the strongest army wins wars. I felt passionately that there was a difference often overlooked by academics pushing the value of ethics. As an adolescent in school, teachers always told me the same thing, "violence is never the answer." As a Marine in the military university teachers always told me the same thing, "America must maintain the ethical high ground in war." I knew my teachers were wrong. But my perspective on violence was more of a philosophy on realism that didn't effectively address the preponderance of America's foreign diplomacy problems. Ultimately, I decided to write a proposal on how to synchronize strategy through a new foreign diplomacy model that enhanced resources rather than wasted them. I felt the United States often bled off advantage through an unsynchronized multiple-government-agency approach. Ironic that I wrote the paper in 2019, and two years later General McKenzie's excuse for the failed Afghanistan evacuation was the seam between the Department of State and Department of Defense.

When researching and writing about synchronizing strategy, I found a very insightful Atlantic Council article titled "All Elements of National Power" addressing the breakdowns within the current foreign diplomacy model.[1] The publication was written by General James Jones, a former commandant of the Marine Corps, and former national security advisor for President Obama. For context, American politicians in the early 2000s, led by Senator John McCain, recognized the need to update the antiquated foreign policy structure created by the 1980s Goldwater-Nichols legislation. Unfortunately, the group never came to a consensus, and the conversation died with John McCain. However, General Jones's recommendations through the process, found in the Atlantic Council article, were directly in line with my paper. At first, I was frustrated when I found General Jones's article. I spent months developing a solution that I thought was a novel idea. As it turned out, like most Americans, I was just uninformed. But after more contemplation, it was reassuring to find someone with his experience recognizing the same problems and proposing similar solutions. As it would happen, a month later General Jones spoke to my class at Command and Staff. He discussed why he departed President Obama's administration prematurely. Ultimately, he claimed irreconcilable differences after President Obama issued a public red line for chemical weapons in Syria and then failed following through.

I found myself agreeing with General Jones again even though we had never met. The military source of power is only an effective deterrent if enemies believe the threat of force. When a president makes a threat and then fails to follow up that threat, the military source of power is significantly marginalized without a single battle ever having been fought. This in turn places a greater demand on the force to validate lethality in future engagements.

It is also interesting to note, that while I conducted my research on foreign diplomacy, Secretary of Defense Mattis publicly resigned over President Trump's policies in Syria. He delivered the resignation paperwork to the media before he gave it to the president. I understood why he made the information public. If Secretary Mattis was convinced the president wouldn't listen privately, the next best thing he could do was to raise the concerns publicly. Perhaps public pressure could convince the president to change course. And as it turned out, President Trump did later change his position on pulling all American military forces from Syria. Thus, it can be argued that Mattis was effective. I'm sure Secretary Mattis studied General John K. Singlaub who commanded military forces in South Korea in 1977. At that time President Carter wanted to pull all the American military forces from Korea. General Singlaub tried to convince President Carter privately that many people would die if the decision was made to pull all American military forces out of Korea. Carter listened but stayed firm in his position to pull American troops out of Korea. General Singlaub then publicly resigned and called out the president's poor choices. The public pressure caused President Carter to change his position. Thus, it can be argued General Singlaub was effective. But if Secretary Mattis imitated this historical example, I wasn't convinced the two scenarios were the same. Secretary Mattis argued to keep troops in a theater to fight against an enemy materializing from twenty years of wars he personally commanded. The entire ISIS situation could have been avoided if Secretary Mattis understood how to link his counterinsurgency theories to a strategic success through a whole-of-government approach. Perhaps that was asking too much. But then again, if the problem couldn't be solved, then maybe he should have been wise enough to pull forces out long ago. Secretary Mattis appeared wrong no matter how I justified it.

Following Command and Staff College, my family and I moved back to Camp Lejeune, where I spent a year at Marine Special Operations Community (MARSOC) as a support battalion executive officer. It was interesting to see behind the curtain. MARSOC perceived itself as a Special Operations Community (SOCOM) asset rather than a Marine Corps asset. Their identity crisis wasn't problematic until MARSOC pursued the Joint Special Operations Community (JSOC). To better explain the dynamic, a person needs to understand the multiple levels of special forces. Most special forces support the combatant commands in the same manner as all other military units. The Goldwater-Nichols legislation of the 1980s created seven geographic combatant commands that in aggregate cover the entire globe. When units deploy, the corresponding combatant commander assumes control of the forces and then assigns missions based on needs and capability. There is one exception to the rule. The highest level of special forces, JSOC, receives tasking straight from the secretary of defense or president. JSOC conducts missions throughout the globe outside the combatant command structure. This is relevant because MARSOC was not a member of JSOC. And General Daniel D. Yoo, the commanding general of MARSOC at the time, wanted to pull back a portion of MARSOC support from combatant command requirements so that he could free up assets and lobby for inclusion into JSOC. He felt this shift would bring more notoriety to MARSOC and distinguish the organization. More prestige meant more money and better recruitment.

I watched the discussion firsthand while attending the MARSOC offsite discussion. Normally executive officers aren't invited to general officer offsites, but my battalion commander was deployed. I was the acting battalion commander at the time; thus I received a ticket to the event by default. At the event, I listened to MARSOC leaders discuss recruitment and training of individuals into MARSOC straight from the civilian world. This discussion centered around finding creative ways to marginalize the leverage the Marine Corps had on MARSOC. There were many appealing reasons for these types of discussions, most notably allowing the organization to pursue goals like JSOC without pushback from the larger Marine Corps. Various leaders at the offsite conveyed that the commandant and the larger Marine Corps were not interested in MARSOC's participation in JSOC. Yet General Yoo, despite understanding the dissent, remained focused on moving MARSOC toward JSOC. However, he never effectively convinced the larger Marine Corps of the vision. Thus, it was no surprise when General Yoo was ultimately told to retire by the commandant following his command. The message was clear: a two-star general who doesn't agree with four-star generals will never become a four-star general. The commandant had selected the next commanding general of MARSOC, who not surprisingly, never mentioned a move to JSOC. Yet even after this event occurred, the Marines of MARSOC still remained entrenched in their position that they worked for SOCOM and not the Marine Corps. The truth was obvious to me all along: if the commandant controls the commander of MARSOC through selection and/or forced retirement, then the commandant will always control MARSOC.

This analogy also applies in a context larger than MARSOC. When senior generals unilaterally decide who gets promoted to their level, the senior generals will always control the type of people leading the military organization. Unfortunately, it is almost impossible for renegade warfighters to penetrate the barriers of the system. Alexander the Great or Elon Musk would never lead the American military in our current system.

While at MARSOC, I was selected to lieutenant colonel. Once selected, the leadership at MARSOC made it clear I needed to find a job elsewhere. The organization was oversaturated with lieutenant colonels, and I counted against their numbers. As a non-badged MARSOC guy—someone who hadn't been through selection and qualified as an operator—I was not a priority. I reached out to 2d Marine Division attempting to find a local job so that my family didn't need to move again. The chief of staff of the division at the time was Colonel Farrell Sullivan. Ironically, Colonel Sullivan went on to pick up general and was the man General McKenzie selected to plan the evacuation in Afghanistan. Colonel Sullivan reviewed my personnel file and decided to make me the 6th Marines regimental operations officer.

I checked into 6th Marines in June 2020. My boss was Colonel Jeffrey Kenney. This tour was very challenging. Colonel Kenney wasn't as openly hostile as my battalion commander in 1/8, but I soon came to realize that all his motivations were summarized by one ambition: how to get a star. This meant as the operations officer, every product I delivered, training event I developed, or meeting I presented always had to be filtered through this context. Additionally, Colonel Kenney's baseline expectation for a regimental operations officer was an eighteen-hour workday. He even specifically stated this at one point, "Stu, I'm going to work you like a slave. I'm going to work you like a dog. And don't expect me to feel bad about that." I very rarely got home that tour to see my children before they went to bed.

There was one time early in our tour together when Colonel Kenney missed a meeting with the commanding general of the division, General Francis Donovan. I had a million things on my plate, and I didn't think managing Colonel Kenney's schedule was my responsibility. If anything, it was the executive officer's responsibility. But I took the face shot nonetheless. I sat in his office as he read back an email from General Donovan. "Jeff, I missed you at the commander's update. Let's stay connected." That was all that was said. But this was devastating to Colonel Kenney. He paced around the office while I sat on the couch. "For him to write this! For a general to say this! For him to spend time to communicate this! We can't allow this to happen again. My staff has failed me." Colonel Kenney was not unique in this reaction. The most important thing to senior officers is their boss's opinion. This seems obvious since officers are only evaluated based on a boss's assessment of performance. Leaders won't get promoted if one boss along the way doesn't like them. But this phenomenon was often distorted into unhealthy behavior. When a senior officer's entire life and ambitions hinged on their boss's opinion, it became such a singular focus that the Marines were an afterthought. Often, the Marines were trained and cared for in the manner that briefed well to the general. The welfare of the Marines become a tool to impress a boss.

All commanding officers state at some point that they want honest feedback. But the truth is that no commanding officer wants honest feedback all the time. There is an art to figuring out the threshold of honest feedback for each commanding officer. A subordinate officer must find the balance between being a pain in the ass and providing honest feedback. I realized very quickly that Colonel Kenney's threshold for honest feedback was very shallow. He pulled me aside multiple times after meetings and lectured me about disagreeing with him openly in meetings. He told me it undermined his authority as the commander.

Colonel Kenney was a tall man. Tall men are statistically promoted more often because people have an unconscious bias that height equates to strong leadership. Colonel Kenney often used his height as a tool of dominance. He would place his hand on my shoulder and physically move me from side to side as if I were a child. He did this to other staff officers as well. At one point he put his hands around the neck of our intelligence officer, Major JC, and acted like he was choking him by literally choking him. When Colonel Kenney walked away, JC was furious. JC was my friend, so I tried to console him the best I could. But JC couldn't let it go. Unfortunately for Colonel Kenney, JC had a special relationship with General Donovan. To understand the deep bond between JC and General Donovan, you need to understand they served together in JSOC. Only a year previously, in 2019, both men had supported the team that killed Abu Bakr al-Bhagdadi, the leader of ISIS at the time. Following the tour at JSOC, both JC and General Donovan transferred to 2d Marine Division. If anyone could call General Donovan directly, it was JC. JC called General Donovan and discussed Colonel Kenney's inappropriate behavior. General Donovan listened to the complaints but ultimately did nothing about it. Despite his credibility in the SOCOM community, General Donovan was as morally weak as all the others. Unfortunately for us, the adjacent regimental commander, Colonel Brian Coyne, also a tall man, was more divisive than Colonel Kenney. If General Donovan wasn't willing to fire Colonel Coyne, he couldn't do anything about Colonel Kenney.

There was another time toward the end of the tour when, late on a Friday night, I walked into Colonel Kenney's office and handed him a product. He asked for minor corrections, so I ran back to my office and updated the product. When I came back to the office, he was talking to his sergeant major. I waited outside the office for twenty minutes and grew impatient. I decided as the operations officer, I had the ability to walk into the office to drop off the completed product on the desk while he spoke to the sergeant major. So I did. I didn't interrupt them, I just walked in, set the products on his desk, and turned to walk out so that I could get home to see my family. As I did Colonel Kenney stopped me. "Hey, Stu. If you ever interrupt me again while I'm talking to my sergeant major, I will fucking cut you in half. I will fucking fillet you. Do you hear me?!" Ironically, the following week I compiled and briefed the regiments annual training statistics on the required bullying training to Colonel Kenney.

Another huge pain during my time as the regimental operations officer was how the DoD addressed COVID. The rules were ludicrous, and they changed daily. Where I spent most of my time at The Basic School discussing equal opportunity, I spent most of my time at the regiment discussing COVID. I never fully understood the different rules governing symptomatic, close contact, or confirmed positive individuals. The default answer was to test a suspected individual and then send them home. If they tested positive, they could return to work after ten days. If they tested negative, they could return to work after fourteen days. Thus, people without COVID who happened to be in the vicinity of people with COVID were isolated for longer periods than the people who tested positive. It raised the question why we even tested the Marines at all. At one point the command tried to be proactive, and we developed a random COVID test to screen across the command similar to a random urinalysis. As a result, the unit became combat ineffective. We isolated more Marines between positives and close contacts than ever before. This did not brief well to the general. We never did that again.

I was also deeply troubled that all the military branches pursued discharges other than honorable for the service members who refused the COVID vaccine. I couldn't wrap my brain around the decision. Senior military leaders consistently preached the obligation to junior service members. Yet, senior leaders were ready to discharge service members who fought in multiple wars with conditions less than honorable because they made an independent medical decision not to be vaccinated. I was also amazed that the Service Chiefs pushed the decision down to subordinate commanders. All refusals were in the same category, so why not make it a Service Policy? The reason was simple: the Service Chiefs were afraid to get dirt on their hands. They pushed the decision down to junior commanders with an unspoken intent of less than honorable. I knew most commanders would go with the flow. They were all too scared to challenge the policy. It would end their career. Their careers were more important than the Service Members.

I was so bothered by the Department of Defense's COVID policies that I started researching Secretary of Defense Lloyd Austin. I knew he was a previous combatant commander and military officer. But when I researched him, I realized he was previously a board member on Raytheon Technologies and Tenet Healthcare, earning nearly $1 million for a handful of meetings. In addition to the money, these are two positions I felt created obvious conflicts of interest. How did we allow general officers to assume board member positions that compromised the service? The companies sought out Lloyd Austin because they knew, even before he was selected to secretary of defense, that a retired general had influence over the active generals. It's insider trading done legally. The only victims are the service members and the American people. But for that same individual to then be selected as the secretary of defense, especially after assuming a board member position with one of the largest government contracting companies, should be bordering on illegal. And, unfortunately, Lloyd Austin isn't unique. Almost all the generals do the same thing. When General Mattis retired from the military he took a board member position at General Dynamics. He gave up the seat when he became the secretary of defense and then he went straight back to his board member position at General Dynamics!

Continuing to research Lloyd Austin, I read that after one hundred days of assuming the office, he came out and made a statement that the biggest threat facing the Department of Defense was COVID. I was dumbfounded. We were in the middle of trying to withdraw from one of the longest wars in American history. Russia was staging military forces on the border of Ukraine. Meanwhile there were obvious systemic issues within the military's culture, progression, training, and procurement. And somehow he came to the conclusion that COVID required the most attention. I decided in that moment that either he didn't understand or he didn't care, but either way he wasn't advocating for the service members in the manner his leadership position demanded.

Another problem not previously discussed deals with the Defense Department's handling of the budget. I understood how broken the system was as a company commander, but my exposure to the broken system hit new heights as a regimental operations officer. Battalion commanders were made to feel shame at the regimental meeting if they hadn't spent enough money. As the fiscal quarters came within a month of completion, if a battalion commander hadn't spent the requisite money, the regiment took the money and gave it to another battalion commander who spent more recklessly. The message was clear: spend faster and quicker and you will get more money.

Furthermore, our procurement ability for basic technology items within the military was filled with bureaucratic red tape. I already inherently understood the problems from my time as The Basic School operations officer. As a result, while in Quantico I developed a special relationship with the head at the Office of Naval Research. Office of Naval Research was able to get modern-day technology for training events under the banner of "testing." They figured out a way to circumvent the entire procurement process. *Why can't we allow a battalion commander to do the same thing?* I always wondered. Office of Naval Research provided basic technology not organic to infantry units if leaders were smart enough to develop a relationship with the organization and put in the requests. While planning a regimental training operation in Camp Lejeune I requested, what I felt, were basic items: robotics, counter unmanned aerial surveillance, video equipment, electromagnetic jamming, unmanned vehicles, and so on. I tried incorporating all the items in my regimental training exercise. But I was told to "pump the brakes" on all the technology, that "we needed to focus on the gear we have."

There isn't a business in the world that could function on that many levels of ineptitude. Yet we allow it, mostly because the money comes from the taxpayer, and no one wants to question the military. But there may be other reasons. The current system prevents fast implementation of technology. Faster implementation would leave general officers behind in their understanding of the battlefield. The slower technology is implemented, the longer those in power maintain control. In the current system, at the

of our specific event, he offered perspective on the larger Marine Corps. "We are in a transitional time in the Marine Corps. We haven't been in a time like this since post-Vietnam. The commandant, General Berger, is restructuring the force the same as Commandants Wilson and Barrow did after Vietnam. His restructuring is critical for victory. The current GWOT generation is not prepared to fight against the Chinese."

Everything about his comments angered me. I was so sick of being told that I wasn't good enough because of...fill in the blank. I wasn't good enough because I hadn't been to Iraq. Then I wasn't good enough because I hadn't been to Afghanistan. Then I wasn't good enough because I wasn't around pre-9/11 for a deeper understanding of unit training. Now I was being told I wasn't good enough to fight the Chinese. And that wasn't all that bothered me about his statement. We were still fighting a war in Afghanistan. Did he forget that? Plus, this wasn't the first story I'd heard about General Wilson's reforms post-Vietnam. I received multiple classes about his greatness. The narrative was always the same, "The drugs, draft, and enlisted service member are the reason we failed in Vietnam." At no point did senior officers ever discuss the numerous failures at the general-officer level. The quintessential case study on moral courage in the military is the My Lai massacre incident in Vietnam, an incident where the United States Army killed unarmed civilians. But an unspoken truth from that case study is that only company grade officers were held accountable. No general officers were held accountable following the incident. From my research, I decided Vietnam is where the American military got off course. The generals failed and then passed the buck on to the junior service member. They were convincing enough that America never reformed the general-officer culture. The closest thing Congress did was pass the Goldwater-Nichols Act, which in many ways, only further empowered the general officer. At no point did we put controls in place for senior military officers winning wars. And now, the generals were running the same play. They were deflecting from their failures. This conversation stuck with me and influenced my later actions.

I moved on from the regimental operations officer that summer. During my time in the billet, I was screened for battalion command. When an officer is screened for command, they are required to fill out a questionnaire. In the questionnaire, officers can RBR (remove by request) if they don't want to be selected to command. There is an alarming number of talented officers who do this. I thought very seriously about submitting an RBR. But my goal at the time was to remain in North Carolina with my family until retirement. I was afraid that if I submitted an RBR the Marine Corps would punish me by giving me orders to another geographic location for my final two years in the service. So I compromised with myself. On the questionnaire, it asked if commanding an operational unit or geographic location was the most important factor. I knew senior officers on the board wanted an officer who stated operational command as the most important factor. But it wasn't the most important factor to me. So, I listed geographic location in North Carolina was more important than operational command. I surmised this slight would most likely result in a non-selection to command, but I rationalized that the Marine Corps would be less likely to punish me with orders to another geographic location if it appeared that I was still screening for command. As it turned out, the Marine Corps gave me exactly what I asked for. They still selected me for command and gave me a nonoperational command on the East Coast. I was selected for Advanced Infantry Training Battalion. It was a perfect fit for me with my background in the infantry and training community. With the selection, I rotated in the summer of 2021.

I assumed command of Advanced Infantry Training Battalion (AITB) on June 25, 2021. My family all came to the change of command ceremony. At this point my boys were ten, nine, and six. They were old enough to start understanding the significance of my military ceremonies. My wife was very excited that I landed the job in North Carolina. She seemed happy. A commanding officer at any unit will work long hours, but AITB had a predictable schedule. We knew I would be able to help with the kids and participate in family functions more than a commander at an operational unit. We also knew the boys were all going to be in the same school for the first time the following school year. My wife was even hired that summer as a teacher at their school. The school was right down the street from our five-bedroom, three-thousand-square-foot house. We had a comfortable and stable life at that time.

The School of Infantry commanding officer, my new boss, was Colonel David Emmel. One of the first times I heard him speak was at my change of command. Colonel Emmel said, "Command should be about service to the Marines." He seemed like an intelligent and educated man. He understood very well how the bureaucracy of the military worked. I paid special attention to how he prepared briefs for General Julian Alford. The first time I sat down with Colonel Emmel in his office, we talked about some of the disciplinary issues within the instructor cadre of the school. I explained to him my previous experience at the School of Infantry as a captain and all the issues I went through with my instructors. I described all the personal problems in their lives coming home from war. But I pointed out the difference in 2021 was that most younger Marines hadn't experienced combat. Only later did I realize that Colonel Emmel somehow never received combat experience. He somehow had never deployed to a twenty-year Afghanistan war over his thirty-year career. I'm sure he was upset with me about that comment. But that would not be the last thing he got upset with me about.

CHAPTER 10:

YOU SHOULD PROBABLY WATCH THE VIDEO— HIT POST. FIRED. ALL IN.

"When even one American who has done nothing wrong is forced by fear to shut his mind and close his mouth then all Americans are in peril."

—Harry Truman

After the suicide attack on the Marines position at the Kabul airfield in Afghanistan, while sitting in my office as the Advanced Infantry Training Battalion commander, I made a video demanding accountability from my senior military leaders. I made the video from my office and debated whether the personal and professional sacrifices were worth the endeavor. Ultimately, I decided someone needed to take a stand. When I got home from work that night, I walked into the house and hit post. I knew once I hit post, there was no going back. Trying not to think about it, I walked over to the aquarium and stared at the turtles. They seemed peaceful. They seemed like they understood their reality better than I did. After sitting with them for thirty minutes, I went upstairs, kissed my kids goodnight, and walked into the bedroom. As I took off my cammies and climbed into bed, my wife walked out of the bathroom and asked, "Did you post a video? Tara told me you posted a video and that you're going viral right now."

"Yes, I posted a video. You need to watch it." She pulled up the video and watched it from a chair in our bedroom. I watched her body language as she watched the video. Her breathing rate increased, her eyes widened, she covered her mouth a couple of times in exasperation. Her body seemed to tense with each word spoken.

When she finished watching, she took a second to collect her thoughts. Then she stared at me lying in the bed. "Wow. You really went for it, huh? I really wish you would have talked to me about this first. Stu, you're going to get us in trouble. You need to take this down. Please take it down."

I could tell she was frightened. And she was right; I should have spoken to her first. But I knew she would have told me the same thing as everyone else. Everyone had different justifications, but the gist was the same: Don't openly challenge your bosses. Even if you are right. The personal and professional cost isn't worth the risk. So, I took a deep breath and answered her, "Babe, there's no taking it down. You can't put the genie back in the bottle once you've made a post like that. But even if I could, I'm not sure I'd want to. I really believe in everything I said."

"What's going to happen to you?" she asked.

"I'll probably be fired," I said.

She studied me when I spoke. She knew me well enough to realize I didn't post the video by mistake. She also absorbed the conviction on my face and realized I was in fact ready to be fired over the video. As she came to grips with the situation, her fear turned to anger. Trying to avoid the fight, I walked downstairs and sat on the couch. While I sat there my phone rang off the hook. I didn't have the energy to answer it. Some of the people who texted were able to get through.

One of the text conversations was with a peer from MARSOC. He texted, "Stu, everyone knows what you said in the video is correct. But it will come at too high of a personal cost. And you're not going to change anything. You need to take the video down."

I responded, "I'm not taking the video down. This is the hill I'm willing to die on. The emperor has no clothes. You must see it."

Then I had one of my instructors text me, "Sir, please take the video down. While I agree with your comments, this could hurt the battalion. I also think these types of statements could be used against us by our enemies. I think you should think about that."

I responded, "If our senior leaders can't address our internal problems, then we shouldn't be talking about our enemies. I'm not taking the video down. You know I appreciate all the instructors in our battalion, but this is bigger than that."

I received over one hundred texts that night and thousands of social media messages. I couldn't possibly respond to all the messages. Many of the messages were from Marines I previously served with stating how proud they were of me. Others pleaded with me to take the video down. There were many comments demanding my resignation. I replied to one of the comments on my LinkedIn page. It is still in the comments portion of my post. "I appreciate your perspective, but I do not plan on resigning. I made a statement I believed to be true. I will allow the investigative process to take place, and I will take accountability for any rules I broke."

That night I stayed on the couch. Despite all the calls and texts, no one from my chain of command contacted me that night. I maybe fell asleep for a couple of hours. It was hard to sleep thinking about the following day. By the time morning rolled around, the video had already been shared forty thousand times and liked by over two hundred thousand people. I knew at that point even the commandant had seen the video.

By the time I showed up to work, my commanding officer had already been looking for me. Within minutes of arriving to my office, he showed up to talk about the video.

"So, you posted a video. I really wish you would have spoken to me first. I think this video is going to be used to create messages that weren't your initial intent."

"Yes, sir. I posted the video, and I acknowledge everything you just said."

"I just don't understand. What were you trying to accomplish with the video? Where do you see this going?"

"I was trying to start a discussion of accountability with our senior leaders. They are failing, and no one is addressing it. I want generals held accountable. I want someone to address them in the same manner you're talking to me. What do I want out of my personal situation? I want to remain the battalion commander of AITB."

"Well, you know how this works. There will be an investigation. Depending on the results of the investigation, I will make a recommendation to General Alford on your future. For now, why don't you take the rest of the weekend off. I'll call you on Monday and give you an update on the situation."

"OK, sir. I'll tie up a couple loose ends with my battalion executive officer, and then I'll go home."

As soon as my boss walked out of my office my executive officer, Major Jay Snelling, walked straight in. Major Snelling wasn't the only Marine watching my office. The entire staff was aware the commanding officer was in my office discussing the video.

"What did he say, sir?"

"He said that I need to take the rest of the weekend off. What do you need from me in terms of turn over?"

"I don't need anything, sir. I just want you to know that we all respect the hell out of you. Our previous battalion gunner called me this morning and said he saw your video. He said he knew that you were going to get in trouble, but he was proud someone finally had the courage to stand up. He got out of the Marine Corps because he couldn't stomach the direction of the service. You reminded him why he joined the Marine Corps."

"Yeah, well, I'll probably get fired over this."

CHAPTER 11:

WHO ARE YOU CALLING CRAZY? —
SECOND VIDEO. SCHOOL BUS. PUBLIC AFFAIRS.

"It is my experience that bold decisions give the best promise of success. But one must differentiate between strategic and tactical boldness and a military gamble... A gamble is an operation which can lead either to victory or to the complete destruction of one's forces. Situations can arise where even a gamble may be justified – as for instance, when in the normal course of events defeat is merely a matter of time, when the gaining of time is therefore pointless and the only chance lies in an operation of great risk."

—General Rommel

I woke up Saturday morning, August 28, feeling hungover even though I didn't drink anything the night before. I had a father-son day planned with my oldest son. I had organized a boat ride around the Outer Banks of North Carolina with him. I thought about cancelling the event, but I had already paid for the boat ride. Plus, I rationalized a day away from the world with a child could be beneficial for my mental health. So, I pulled myself out of bed and walked downstairs. The kids were on the couch watching a cooking show. I sat with them, drinking my coffee, thinking about how to tell them their father had been fired. And more importantly what it meant for them; I probably wouldn't be living with them for the next three years. I remembered the comment from my children the last time I had geo-bachelored: "Last year we didn't have a father."

"Hey, guys, turn off the TV. We need to have a family meeting. There is something I need to tell you guys." They were annoyed that I interrupted their TV programming, but they knew whenever they heard "family meeting" it was typically something important. I looked over at my wife in the kitchen. "Do you want to come to the meeting?" I asked her.

"No. This is your news." Her tone signaled to the kids that I was about to tell them something she was angry about. They stared at me.

"Guys, do you remember two months ago when you came to the change of command ceremony for my new job? Well, I was fired from that job yesterday. I wasn't fired for doing a bad job at work. I was fired because I made a video saying something that I thought was right. But it upset a lot of people. So, I don't work there anymore."

My second son immediately pieced together the implication. "Are we going to move again?" he asked.

"No. Your dad may be sent to Quantico for a little while, but I'll still come home on the weekends just like we did before. You will get to stay here. Nothing changes for you guys."

"Wow. I'm sorry, Dad. That's not fair that you were fired for doing the right thing," said my oldest son.

"Thanks, buddy. OK, you can guys can go back to watching your cooking show."

A couple hours later my oldest son and I got in my truck and drove to the Outer Banks of North Carolina. He and I had a great day together on the boat. I intentionally left my phone in the truck so that I could completely disconnect and focus on him. Leaving my phone in the truck also meant that we didn't have a camera, so we only have memories of the wild horses, sea turtles, sand dollars, and smiles. When we finished the boat ride we got back in the truck and drove to an Airbnb house we had rented on the beach. We ordered a pizza and, sticking with the sea theme, watched a marathon of shark movies. My son finally got tired after the third movie and went off to bed.

Curiosity killed the cat. When my son went off to bed, I pulled my phone out for the first time that day. I started scrolling through social media. I noticed people were setting up accounts and pretending to be me. All the fake social media accounts used my pictures and name to criticize President Biden. The narrative started developing that this was about politics. Everyone assumed I spoke against President Biden. Did they listen to my video? I never once mentioned the president's name. It was clear to me the general officers had failed. I also noticed GoFundMe pages created under my name. I didn't ask anyone to fundraise for me. I didn't want people thinking my actions were a ploy for money.

I continued scrolling through comments. I started reading a conversation about the utility of an active-duty officer speaking out while in uniform…and boom…that's when I saw it.

Colonel Hobbs had commented on my LinkedIn page, "If Stuart Scheller was honorable, he would resign." My anxiety gripped me as I processed the comment. After everything I had been through with this man. We both jumped on a grenade together to protect a SNCO. The words I used in the video, "Throw your rank on the table," reflected something he'd taught me. He knew those were his words. When he wrote the article about the racist Marine Corps, I called and asked if he was all right because I cared about him. But he didn't show the same empathy. He chose not to call or email after he knew I had been fired. Instead, he chose to get on my social media and publicly challenge my honor without clarifying any context about our relationship. He decided to attack me when I was most vulnerable. It felt like finding out my wife had cheated on me. I threw my phone across the room.

I went back to my bedroom and laid on the bed. Again, I couldn't sleep. After all my service to the country, this was how they were going to treat me? Everyone was turning on me. I gave my whole life to the organization, and still not a single leader addressed the content of my statements. Instead, they attacked me from all angles. Did I really want to geo-bachelor again? Did I want to be away from my family for another three years? Did I want to hide in a cubicle and limp toward retirement for the next three years of my life? Did the Marine Corps care about me as much as I cared about the organization?

I started thinking about Afghanistan. American military leaders conducted a withdrawal in the peak fighting season with the Taliban. They abandoned Bagram Air Base. They left five thousand prisoners in the base for the Taliban. They allowed the Taliban to push from Pakistan through the entire country of Afghanistan. Americans were then forced to deal with the Taliban for external security before the evacuation was complete. Obviously, the Taliban allowed the suicide bomber through their checkpoint, which resulted in the deaths of thirteen service members. At a bare minimum, senior leaders owed an acknowledgment of failure so that the organization could heal and evolve. I then thought back to General Jurney's comments about the military's pivot. Senior leaders were already developing a narrative about the failures of the GWOT generation narrowly focused on war's tactical level as they restructured for China and Russia. I concluded that they weren't ever going to address their failures. Someone needed to challenge them. Someone needed to speak the truth.

I hadn't planned on resigning, but Saturday night, August 28, I realized I was in a war with the Marine Corps. I believed General McKenzie should have convinced the president to keep more troops in Afghanistan until after the evacuation. If he was unable to convince the president, then he should have gone public with his position and resigned to prevent failure. General Singlaub had the courage and insight to publicly challenge a president. Instead, General McKenzie remained silent and, as he later stated, "obeyed the orders." But his choice to remain silent after accepting unrealistic restraints didn't abdicate him of accountability.

That night I began strategizing for the first time. Reflecting back, it is clear that chess impacted my thinking. Chess was an outlet. It challenged my mind when I needed more intellectual stimulation. I played chess on my phone at home, in the car, and even at work while pretending to listen to annual training. I always played queen out opening. It was a much more aggressive approach than standard openings. I preferred forcing an opponent's response to my actions. In that vein, I realized I needed to apply pressure on the Marine Corps and force them to react. *How can I do that?* I thought. *If the generals won't hold themselves accountable, and the political leaders won't hold them accountable, maybe all that leaves is us...the American people.* Ironic, because when I posted the first video, I signed it "US." I did so intentionally as a double meaning for United States, and the people...us. I had read the Declaration of Independence many times. The Founding Fathers' statement I always focused on was how the power of the government came from the people. The document also stated when any American form of government stops working for the people, it is the people's obligation to throw off that form of government. *Was it that bad?* I thought. *Can the system be reformed, or do we need to throw off the current form of government?* I came to three conclusions that night. First, any perceived power I had from my social media platforms came from the American people. Not the American military. Second, I was going to resign. And I was going to do so very publicly. And third, the American system of government was deeply flawed. I felt fundamental changes were required.

I woke up the next morning, took my son to breakfast, and drove him back to the house. It was Sunday, August 28. When I got home, I asked my wife if I could head out to my farm for the afternoon. I told her I needed some time alone. "Of course, babe," she said. "Take all the time you need." I wanted to tell her I had already decided to resign. But I knew in my soul that she would passionately protest. Once she protested, I'd be back in the same dilemma, except, if I spoke to her and then resigned regardless, she'd be even more angry. She also would never approve of me making another video. But I decided going public again was the only way to keep pressure on the broken system. I was taking risks involving the entire family, but I wasn't asking her about it.

My "farm" was nothing more than a fifty-acre tract of land filled with North Carolina pine trees. In 2012, I moved my mutual fund investments into the purchase of the land. I viewed it as an investment I could also enjoy. I leased the land to a veteran nonprofit organization called AHERO (American Heroes Enjoying Recreation Outdoors). The organization focused on treating veterans for PTSD with outdoor therapy. I participated in some of the events AHERO had at my farm. I quickly realized that we needed a small cabin or some place to speak out of the weather. Without a lot of money, I decided to buy a school bus and refurbish it.

I drove out to the farm so that I had a quiet place to make a video. I knew the school bus was the perfect place. When I got to the farm, the only thing I staged was a chess board in the camera shot. I used my standard opening. Queen pawn out then bishop immediately threatens knight. I typically killed a knight with a bishop in the beginning of every game. I found it helped disrupt an enemy's early formation. When an enemy's original plans are disrupted, the rest of the game is less scripted, and mistakes are more common. Then I set my cell phone on a wooden Indian, sat in a chair, and made my second video. I only made one take.

I started the video by stating my name and location, on an abandoned school bus in eastern North Carolina. I stated that I appreciated all views on my social media, "even the people who think I should have handled it differently. I think the debate is healthy." I knew the emotional moment of declaring my resignation was the point of the video, so I tried clarifying some information in the first half of the video. First, I addressed the fake social media accounts and GoFundMe pages under my name. Then I discussed my wife. "After I post this video, my wife, I love you, you're a great mother, you've been down for the cause the last seventeen years, and I don't know what decisions you're going to make in the next seventy-two hours." I knew deep down the second video could lead to a divorce. So, I publicly stated her Venmo and PayPal addresses. I figured if she left me after I gave up our retirement, perhaps Americans could raise money for her and the kids. I also addressed Colonel Hobbs. I explained my relationship with him. I referred to the missing machine gun optic situation indirectly, stating that "we went through some very challenging things together." I added, "And after he left the Marine Corps, he's started a lot of controversy by talking about racial diversity and equal opportunity problems in the Marine Corps. And from that respect I have disagreed with him. But just because we have different opinions doesn't mean I don't respect him. Sir, I love you like a father."

I continued. "I want to make the announcement, today after seventeen years, I'm currently not pending legal action, and I could stay in the Marine Corps for another three years, but I don't think that's the path I'm on. I'm resigning my commission as a United States Marine officer effective immediately." I couldn't remain in an organization refusing to acknowledge failure. "All I asked for was accountability of my senior leaders when there are clear, obvious mistakes that were made. I'm not saying we can take back what has been done. All I'm asking for is accountability. For people to comment on what I said, and to say yes, mistakes were made. And had they done that, I would have gone back into rank and file, submitted, and accomplished what I wanted."

The school bus was normally a place where veterans discussed their experiences in Iraq and Afghanistan. It felt like an appropriate place to state, "I want senior leaders to accept accountability. I think them accepting accountability would do more for service members with PTSD and struggling with purpose than any other transparent piece of paper or message. And I haven't received that." I then itemized the millions of dollars I forfeited by resigning three years prior to retirement. "I think that money should go back to all the senior general officers because I think they need it more than I do. Because when I'm done with what I'm about to do, you all are going to need the jobs and the security." I took a deep breath and then continued, "I want to be clear that I love the Marine Corps." I repeated Colonel Hobbs's comment again, visibly emotional at this point, "'If Stuart Scheller were honorable he would resign.' You have no idea what I'm capable of doing."

I ended the video by saying, "The one thing they don't tell you is that going after stability and money can make you a slave to the system. And it can make you compromise what you truly believe in. I don't need a single dollar." My final statement was, "Follow me, and we will bring the whole fucking system down. I am honorable, and you can ask any Marine who served with me the last seventeen years. I dare you to ask them all and find out what I'm made of." I then shook my head in disgust and said, "We're just getting started."

I couldn't even bring myself to watch the video after I recorded it. I was too emotional. I just wanted to hit post and not think about it this time, but I had terrible service on the farm. I drove fifteen minutes to the town of New Bern, where I sat in a Starbucks and posted the second video to my LinkedIn and Facebook pages. When I hit post, the texts and calls immediately came pouring back in. One of the texts were from Colonel Emmel. I began to call him back, but before I could, Lieutenant Colonel Mike Mannochio, the SOI executive officer, called me first. I answered the call.

"Hey, Stu, how you doing?"

"I just posted another video. I'm sure it's going to create more work for you."

"Don't worry about that right now. Where are you? I want to come pick you up."

"I'm in New Bern. Look, I'm not suicidal. I don't need you to pick me up."

"Do you have any guns?"

"Yes, of course I have guns, Mike. I'm a fucking infantry officer."

"Let me come meet you."

"That's not necessary."

"I'm worried about you. Can you come to my house?"

"Look, Mike, I answered your phone call out of professional courtesy. I'm not suicidal. I don't work for you, and you don't outrank me. I'm not meeting you or telling you where I'm at. The CO just texted me too; please tell him that if he needs me, he can order me to show up to work. Other than that, I'll see you on Monday morning." Then I hung up. Mike later acknowledged this conversation in the investigation. He stated I was rude and hung up on him. How many times can you explain you're not suicidal before getting frustrated?

I got in my car and started driving back to my house. I was not looking forward to the conversation with my wife. While I was driving, Colonel Hobbs was one of the hundred people who called me. I guess he still had my phone number after all. I silenced the call. He left a voicemail that I later played at my court-martial.

Colonel Hobbs voicemail said, "Stu, look I know you don't want to talk to me right now, but I think you have PTSD. I'm worried about you. We're all worried about you. You fucked up big time by posting to social media. I was just talking to General Neller [the former commandant] about you. It's not too late. If you get on your knees and fucking beg for mercy, you may be able to keep your retirement."

Get on my knees and fucking beg for mercy, huh? How quickly I went from the guy with no honor to the crazy guy. At what point was he going to address his faults or the content of my statements? I wondered if he ever really cared about me or if his previous sacrifices on my behalf were only about protecting himself. Even in my time of despair, I still found irony in his name. Col Thomas

Hobbs. I don't know why his parents chose that name, but it was hard not to recognize the parallel to Thomas Hobbes of the 1600s who wrote the book *Leviathan*. The Leviathan was the social contract between the citizen and the government. Thomas Hobbes of the 1600s wrote his book during the same time as the Treaty of Westphalia. The Treaty of Westphalia moved the world from the medieval religious dominated monarchies to the nation-state model dominating the globe today. An unspoken truth underpinning the current model is that the nation-state maintains a monopoly on violence. Thomas Hobbes of the 1600s wrote the *Leviathan* because he believed the government needed absolute control to keep men accountable. But I knew the Thomas Hobbes of the 1600s and the Thomas Hobbs of the 2000s were both wrong. All humans were both good and evil. All governments comprised of humans possessed both good and evil intentions. The secret resided in balance. The government needed to hold the man accountable just as the man needed to hold the government accountable. In the end, I felt strongly that a man pursuing a just cause should never beg for mercy from a centralized power demanding absolute authority.

As I continued to drive, someone sent me a screenshot of my face on the school bus as the banner video for Fox News. My story was now immediately getting picked up by all the news stations. I was even getting coverage in the liberal media like CNN. The entire nation was watching my saga unfold.

My wife was waiting for me by the time I got home. "I know you posted another video. We need to speak," she said. We went in the backyard so it was harder for the kids to listen. They could sense the tension all over our faces, so as we spoke, we watched their faces peeking at us through the glass sliding door. "I established clear boundaries that I didn't want you posting another video. You didn't listen to me. And again, you did something compromising our safety without speaking to me. I don't understand what's going on with you. This isn't you. You are so smart. Why would you throw away everything we've worked for?"

"I know it looks crazy. But it's not. I need to apply pressure on them. I have a plan. I need you to trust me. Can you trust me?"

"I don't think I can trust you anymore. I need you to leave."

Hearing that my wife couldn't trust me anymore was deeply troubling. I stormed upstairs and hastily packed an overnight bag. When I got in my truck and began to back the truck out of the driveway, my wife stood at the doorway. This memory will be burned into my mind for eternity. She was crying and waving goodbye. I think somewhere deep inside us, we both knew she was waving goodbye to our marriage. I cried all the way to the motel thinking about it.

I found a cheap motel in Jacksonville, North Carolina. I figured I might be there a while, so I didn't want an expensive room. The establishment indirectly targeted divorced parents, poor people, and drug addicts. As I sat in my room mindlessly scrolling through the TV my phone continued to ring off the hook. I monitored who was calling to ensure it wasn't anyone important. I answered my parents' phone call. "Stu, we are worried about you. We are coming up to North Carolina."

"No. That's not what I want. I don't want to see anyone. Please don't come up."

"We are coming. We don't have to see you, but we want to be there." *Great, just when I thought I couldn't be any more stressed out.*

I also got a phone call from my friend Lieutenant Colonel Jeff Cummings. Jeff was another infantry officer who had served with me in 3/2 as a company commander. He had recently graduated the School of Advanced Warfighting in Quantico and moved back to Camp Lejeune to be an operational planner for General Donovan in 2d Marine Division. Since his family had moved back to North Carolina that summer, our families had hung out multiple times. I considered us good friends. I answered his phone call, "What's up man. What do you need."

"Hey, I'm out here at your farm. Where are you."

"I'm not at the farm Jeff. Go home. I'm fine."

"You're not going to tell me where you're at. Ok, man. Well Naval Criminal Service Investigators are looking for you.

"Obviously I have my phone on. Tell them to be smart enough to call or text. Again, I'm fine, I'm not suicidal."

"Well one other thing before you hang up. I'm not sure if you're talking to her, but Jackie and the kids left the house. We helped her and the kids leave. I'm watching your turtles. There was a bunch of media showing up to the house."

"Ok. Thanks for doing…all of that. You're a good friend." When I got off the phone Jeff continued to text me.

"What's the bigger purpose of all this? What's your plan? I know you're not crazy, I'm just trying to figure out what you're trying to accomplish?" I mostly ignored his follow-up texts without thinking too much about them.

Then another lieutenant colonel Marine Corps friend texted also saying NCIS was looking for me. I started getting frustrated. "Tell them to stop calling all my friends. All they have to do is call me. Or they can show up to my work tomorrow morning and speak with me. But this is ridiculous." As soon as I got off the phone someone texted me a statement released by the Marine Corps public affairs team. "We are aware of the second video posted by Lieutenant Colonel Scheller. We are currently trying to locate him to ensure he is not a threat to himself or to others."

What…the…fuck? I thought. *I've had my phone on the whole day. I already spoke to my command today. I've answered calls and texts from all the friends who might have been worried.* The Marine Corps wasn't trying to find me. They were trying to publicly discredit me. This is where I started to understand the misguided reach of the Marine Corps Communications Directorate. They seemed to protect the Marine Corps over the welfare of the individual Marine. It was clear after reading the Marine Corps' public position they were going to start attacking my mental health. I laid in bed the rest of the night thinking about my next moves. Would the command order a mental health evaluation? I'm sure they needed validation that I was crazy. Was I crazy? Was I expecting too much from my leadership? I didn't think so...but then again...does a crazy person know they're crazy? I hoped I was strong enough to stand up to their scrutiny. As I continued to play hypotheticals through in my mind, I listened to a young Marine having sex with what I imagined was a stripper in the room next to me. Listening to her scream made me laugh despite everything going on at that point. *Semper Fi Mother Fucker (SFMF)*, I thought and then drifted off to sleep.

CHAPTER 12:

IT WAS A METAPHOR—
HOSPITAL. LAWYERS. MEDIA.

*"Successful companies tend to develop a bias for pre-
dictability and stability; they work on defending what
they have. Change is tempered by the fear that there is
much to lose. The organization at all levels filters out
information that would suggest new approaches, mod-
ifications, or departures from the norm. The internal
environment operates like an immune system to isolate
or expel 'hostile' individuals who challenge current di-
rections or established thinking. Innovation ceases; the
company becomes stagnant; it is only a matter of time
before aggressive competitors overtake it."*[2]

—Michael Porter, "The Competitive Advantage of
Nations," *Harvard Business Review*

I woke up at 06:30 on Monday August 30 and scrolled through all
the news channels before heading into work. I wasn't the banner
story, but my story was still hanging on the major network web-
sites. On CNN, an article about me was underneath a picture of

General Donahue, the commanding general of the 82nd Airborne Division who responded to the self-induced Afghan disaster. The picture showed him strutting up to the plane as the last military member in Afghanistan. The war was over. At that time, everyone celebrated his picture as a symbol of victory. All I could see was another hypocrite. We probably had a public affairs team taking pictures with a pre-spun narrative to deflect our surrender to the Taliban. Who celebrates themselves after a failure like that? Unfortunately, the military had figured out how to weaponize the media, and that's how they spun it. Months later I spoke to an Army soldier from the 82nd Airborne who conducted the Kabul Airfield perimeter security with General Donahue. He confirmed General Donahue ordered his soldiers to conduct a police call (cleanup) of the base before turning it over to the Taliban. In a deeply sickening way, I knew it to be true. That's how far we've drifted.

I arrived at my new temporary office within eyeshot of my commanding officer at 08:00. An extremely overweight O-4 Naval doctor waited for me. He was nervous. Not only did I outrank him, but I think I also scared him. He walked into my office, closed the door, and sat down so that we could speak.

"Doc, before you even start speaking, I want you to listen to me very carefully. First, I'm not suicidal. Second, I'm not a threat to any person. Third, I'm not allowing you to evaluate me any further unless the commanding officer orders a mental health evaluation. Now get out of my office."

"OK, sir," he said and exited the room as quickly as he had entered. He walked into the commanding officer's office and closed the door. I sat at my desk and stared at Colonel Emmel's door wondering how he would play this.

Ten minutes later Colonel Emmel walked out of his office with the doctor behind him. He handed me a piece of paper. "I was hoping you would volunteer for a mental health evaluation. But since you refuse, I'm formally ordering you to get a mental health evaluation."

"Sir, the Marine Corps never made me get a mental health evaluation when I missed the birth of my son, when I came home from my combat deployments, or after I killed people. Only when I questioned leadership. What does that tell you?"

He didn't answer my question. Instead, he chose to talk logistics. "I want Lieutenant Colonel Mannochio and Lieutenant Colonel Lane escorting you to the hospital." After he walked back into his office, my escorts surrounded me and walked me to a van already waiting outside. We piled into the van. One of my escorts sat in front of me, and the other one sat behind me.

When we arrived, the hospital was already waiting for me. They pulled me into the psych ward immediately. My escorts were told they needed to wait outside. They did allow the fat doctor from SOI accompany me back to my hospital bed. The nurse came in and took my vitals. "Your blood pressure is kind of high. Does it normally run high?"

"No," I said in a tone that I hoped would signal the uniqueness of the situation without follow-up questions. "OK, well the doctor will be in shortly," she said and walked out.

The doctor was my age. I couldn't see his rank, but I assumed we were probably the same rank. "Lieutenant Colonel Scheller. You are all over the news. I actually didn't know who you were until the nurses just told me. I watched your most recent video. Anything you want to tell me about it?"

I knew his opinion was very important. I couldn't be too emotional. I very slowly and deliberately spoke. "Doc, I really appreciate you taking the time to speak with me. I have great respect for the work you do. I've sent many people to this exact place who needed the help. But I should not be here. I believe I was sent here as a means to discredit me. But I will answer any questions that you have."

"Based on your experience, do you think there was anything you said in that video that warrants your command sending you here?"

"I said I was going to bring the whole fucking system down. It was meant as a metaphor for the corruption within the system. It wasn't a direct threat on any person or place."

"OK, so are you a threat to yourself or others?"

"I am not a threat to myself or others."

The rest of the conversation was superficial. There was a short check of my vitals, and he quickly glanced over my body. Before he walked out he said, "Hey, I don't think you're crazy. I'd offer you a bed here to sleep because it looks like you really need it. But I don't think you'll take it. Here's my number; please text if you need anyone to speak with. Good luck on the path you're heading down."

"Thanks, doc. And no, I don't want your bed. I've got a resignation package to submit," I said allowing myself to smile. Then we walked out of the hospital. My lieutenant colonel escorts were still waiting on us. We all piled back in the van and drove back. No words were spoken the entire time. I kept thinking about the new dynamic with my peers. I was trying to help the Marine Corps. But these officers were so conditioned by the bureaucracy, so dependent on the system, they were willing to attack me to protect it. If every senior officer believed I was crazy and I was the only one with a different thought process, maybe in a sense I did fit the definition of crazy.

I walked back into the office. Colonel Emmel was waiting on me. He was obviously displeased that I wasn't admitted. I was obviously displeased that he had challenged my mental health. We stared at each other in his office for a moment before he spoke and addressed the awkwardness. "Stu, I had to make sure you were OK. Now that were past that, we can move forward with your resignation. I will have the executive officer help you submit your resignation. My priority for you is completing your checkout process. I need you to turn in all your gear, get your final physical done, and complete the transition-readiness seminar. I'm also going to start formally documenting the warnings I give you about your conduct on social media. I want you to re-sign a formal document stating you understand the Marine Corps policy on social media."

I signed his document, walked out of the office, and pretended to work. I actually sat in my office and wrote another post. I posted it an hour later. It is still hanging on my social media:

> When I went into work this morning, I was ordered by my commanding officer to go to the Hospital for a mental health screening. I was evaluated by the mental health specialists and then sent on my way. My CO is a standup guy, and I understand why he did it, but it brings up a couple of important issues:
>
> First, excusing the actions of service members because of "PTSD" does more damage to service members than any trauma in combat. I have been in very traumatic combat situations. But because of that I am STRONGER. Post traumatic growth. If you're worried about someone…you should reach out and check on them. But never excuse a service member's actions with a wave of the hand to PTSD. You are crippling them by failing to hold them accountable. And for the people who checked on me after my last video…I'm sorry if I scared you. But know that despite my emotions, my words are always carefully thought out. Second, as stated in previous posts, accountability from senior leaders would alleviate feelings of guilt or shame in service members more than individual counseling. It would save thousands of lives. On May 6th Secretary of Defense Lloyd Austin said, "the most immediate threat [to the DoD] is COVID." According to the 2020 National Veteran Suicide Prevention Annual Report the number of Veteran suicide deaths documented in 2018 was well over

6,000. And the numbers continue to rise. From a statistical perspective, it's pretty easy to argue that COVID isn't the biggest threat. Third, for all my followers…I'm not going anywhere. Everyone is scared that the weight of the system is crashing down on me. But I know something you don't… it's the system that's going to break. Not me.

I am moving forward with my resignation. I, like many of you, am very scared. But courage isn't the absence of fear, it's the ability to overcome it. At the end of the day, if I stand with accountability and integrity, the system can't beat me.

We can't ALL be wrong.

They only have the power because we allow it.

Every generation needs a revolution.

Bxf6

Bxf6 was a chess move. Bishop kills knight. Disrupt their opening moves. Apply pressure on the system. After I made the post, Major Tyler Brummond, the Marine lawyer who had called me on Monday, knocked on my door. "Sir, we spoke on Monday. If you have a couple of minutes, I'd really like to speak with you."

"You can have a couple minutes, Tyler. Come on in the office."

"I think you broke multiple rules with the second video. I think you need to stop making statements. The Marine Corps is going to press charges against you."

"Is that it?"

"You don't need to resign. And you don't need to use me as your lawyer, but you need to get a lawyer."

"Since we are offering advice, here's some for you. You don't need a law degree to understand the law. I know what rules I broke. I question the utility of your higher-level degree if you can't see the bigger picture. Your two minutes are up. Thanks for stopping by."

He got up and left. I don't think he'd ever been told something like that by a potential defendant before. In hindsight I shouldn't have spoken to him like that, but I was in attack mode at that point. I stayed in my office until 16:00 that day. My boss asked to speak with me, but he had been in his office speaking to someone on the phone, presumably about me, for hours so I figured we could speak in the morning. I went back to the motel and started drinking. Drinking, thinking, drinking, reading, drinking, thinking. I spoke to multiple reporters through my ring doorbell camera. "Can we please just have five minutes of your time? I flew all the way in from New York."

"I didn't ask you to fly in. I stated on my social media I wasn't speaking to media. Go away." I eventually drifted off with Miller Lite cans all over the room.

I woke up the next morning feeling hungover. When I drove onto base the gate guards recognized me. "Holy shit, it's you. Sir, I just want to tell you that we all support you. You are our hero. Thanks for speaking for us." I nodded at the sergeant and continued driving onto base.

When I came into work Colonel Emmel immediately walked into my office. "I thought I told you I wanted to speak to you yesterday. I watched you walk to your truck and leave early."

"I left at 16:00. You said you wanted to speak with me at 14:30. Then you were on the phone for almost two hours. I assumed it was about me. I assumed we could speak about it today, or if it was important enough, you would call me."

"From now on, you are going to sit in this office. I don't want you using the bathroom or eating lunch without talking to the executive officer. This office is your appointed place of duty."

"With the task list you've given me, I could complete everything from home. But instead you gave me an office next to yours so you could monitor me like a child. You were watching me out the window? This feels illegal. I'm not on restriction. I'm not pending legal action. You can't keep me as a prisoner in here."

"You're a Marine officer. I shouldn't have to monitor you like this. But here we are. You will be here every day from 0800 to 1700. You are not to go anywhere without checking out with the executive officer. Am I clear?"

"I acknowledge your position, sir." It was the second time I had answered his question with the word "acknowledgment." I wanted him to feel like, even though I understood what he wanted, I might break the rules anyways. Officers aren't paid to follow the rules. They are paid to know when not to follow the rules. As soon as he left my office, I submitted my resignation paperwork.

I debated between a long, scathing letter or a short, concise message. I decided to keep it short and to the point. I requested a resignation date of September 11, 2021. I knew the requested date was arbitrary. I would ultimately be processed out as fast as the system allowed. Any date I listed was irrelevant, but they still required it, so I listed September 11, 2021. The symbolism seemed appropriate. President Biden used that date to drive a hasty plan. Why couldn't I use that date to drive a hasty resignation? I ended the letter with, "My reason for submitting a letter of resignation: A lack of trust and confidence in your ability to lead." I was so angry when I signed the letter that I accidently poked a hole in the signature line. My executive officer kicked it back because of the small hole. I printed, signed, and handed him another copy. I then walked outside with the copy he refused to accept. I took a picture of it and posted it to my social media.

The rest of the week was very challenging for me. It was one of the hardest times of my life. Whether I was sitting in my temporary office or my motel room, I was completely isolated. Colonel Emmel told me General Alford would assign an investigating officer by the end of the week. I made a post about it. Ironically, it's the only post the investigating officer didn't include in my investigation. I guess he didn't want to illustrate how close I came to predicting the truth. That Wednesday afternoon, I wrote:

> The Marine Corps will assign an investigating officer. Most likely a Colonel. In his investigative capacities, the Colonel will write an unnecessarily long document, with 323 findings of facts. He will ultimately find my posts/statements in violation of 2 to 3 UCMJ articles. Then, on page 38 of the investigation, he will "recommend further administrative action." Once the investigating officer finalizes his recommendation, the Marine Corps will decide if they should pursue court martial. Normally they would (and should), but this situation may be different. If it does go to court martial, I will be found guilty, and will probably do some jail time. This will provide me a valuable opportunity to read, write, and contemplate.... Young officers don't join to become yes men. Young aspirational politicians don't join to compromise their values. IT'S THE SYSTEM. The system forces us to give small pieces of ourselves so that we can continue playing. We are willing to give up these pieces believing it will lead to a place within the system where we eventually "influence real change." The problem is, that over time, those small pieces add up to significant moral, spiritual, mental, and physical changes. The system changes people, and they don't even realize it.

That night I went back to my motel room. Two captains I knew texted me that the commandant had addressed my case in a speech to their Expeditionary Warfare School that afternoon. They said a captain asked about social media and how the Marine Corps could prevent people using it to discuss political views or challenge leadership. Thus, without using my name directly, the commandant started addressing my situation.

"You can't get on social media and criticize the president without it ending at court-martial."

"That's bullshit," I texted back to the captains. I never spoke about the president. The commandant was obviously referencing the fake social media accounts under my name. He was projecting crimes upon me that weren't true. It was the definition of undue command influence. So, I made another post. It stated:

General Berger/Sir,

I understand you want to court martial me. Your entire staff has already told me. All the Captains you spoke to today already texted me. You recently banned all unit social media pages so that you could centralize the message. Because, I'm assuming, you think Marine leaders aren't capable of passing a message in line with your intent. Your problem right now...is that I am moving faster than you. I'm out maneuvering you. Where can we find this philosophy...

C4

C4 was another chess move. Pawn to the center. Always control the center of the board. I ended up deleting both posts later in the week. But the post to the commandant still made it into my investigation. Interesting to note, that when the investigating officer placed this post into the investigation, he cut out "You recently banned all unit social media pages to that you could centralize the message. Because, I'm assuming, you think Marine leaders aren't capable of passing a message in line with your intent." Perhaps he thought that part of the message made too much sense, or maybe he just thought I sounded more crazy without the logical part of the argument. My wife called me the same night. I wasn't prepared to speak with her. I silenced the phone call.

The following morning, Thursday, September 2, I didn't know it at the time, but Mrs. Chaudhry, a civilian who works in the communications directorate, sent out her weekly summary entitled "The CMC Wrap-Up," to General Berger and the senior generals. I figured this out later because they put the email in my investigation. She stated in that specific email:

> There have been 1.1k articles, receiving 1.4 million total engagement related to LtCol Stuart Scheller's video, demanding accountability among senior leaders. It also has 2.9 billion potential reach, which represents the number of individual users who could have seen the content at various points throughout the day. 77.5% articles are neutral, 21.1% negative and 1.4% positive. The negative articles focus on being critical of the military for relieving LtCol Scheller for his video demanding accountability and stating there needs to be an investigation into how the events of Afghanistan have been handled to hold senior military leaders accountable. Communications Directorate is running the following campaign to counter the narrative, "There is a forum in which Marine leaders can address their disagreements with the chain of command, but it's not social media." This narrative was able to affect the sentiment with many

of the articles, with 17% of the overall articles including the statement.

Meanwhile, at SOI, I went into work and asked Colonel Emmel for leave. "Sir, I'm having problems with my family. I really need some time away to speak with my wife."

"No, Stu," he said. "You can't take leave until your out-processing is complete. That is your priority."

Getting more frustrated, I made another post that day. The relevant portion stated:

> Sooooooo let's summarize my current position: My family left me. I've given up my retirement...I'm pending court martial and depending on the outcome...potential brig time. And now my motel room is starting to smell like empty miller light cans because maids don't clean in covid.

I regretted posting that. Immediately everyone started asking about my family. I deleted the post only an hour after posting it. I had potentially painted my wife in a negative manner because I was mad at Colonel Emmel. I needed her back.

That night when I left work, someone sent me a statement General Berger made that week addressing the situation in Afghanistan. He stated:

> While it's relatively fresh in our minds, we need the honest, open critique, or a commission...that cracks open: What were the options that were available, who made what decisions at what time? We need to try to figure out a framework or how can we study, to your point, what went right, what went wrong, what can we learn going forward.

Was that it? Was that all we were going to get? I wondered. What he didn't state publicly was that orders were put out across the force not to comment, like, or engage my posts in any manner. The entire military started doing small group–directed training to spin the narrative about the inappropriateness of my actions. The power of the organization seemed overwhelming. I didn't go back to the motel. I aimlessly drove around Jacksonville, North Carolina, crying. I got out of my truck, and in my pain, posted a picture of my crying face begging my wife to take me back.

> Jackie, I am so sorry. I haven't cried until today. When my rage left, I was only filled with sadness. And those feelings were only because you weren't here. You didn't leave me, I asked you to leave with the kids. Because I felt you didn't understand. I felt like nobody understood. I never needed the Marine Corps. But I've always needed you. If you'll take me back, I'll spend the rest of my life making it up to you…somehow. Bartaflickle.

Baraflickle was a code word from an old Miller Lite commercial. I said in the post that she hadn't left me, that I had left her. This statement was directed at the rest of the world. We both knew she had asked me to leave, but it wasn't fair that I made the comments publicly. I thought this version might help correct the problem. But as it turns out, it's hard to fix one mistake with another mistake. When she left town, she deactivated her FaceBook. I knew she'd reactivate it to see the post. I had a friend text the post to Jackie to expedite the process. I watched on my FaceBook as her account reactivated. For context, in the information part of my FaceBook, her picture disappeared from my marriage status when she deactivated her account. I used this as an indicator. Within twenty minutes of my post, I watched her picture show back up in the marriage portion of my information section. I watched as she kept her account active for thirty minutes and then deactivated it again. I believe that was the last time her FaceBook account was active. I deleted the post as soon as she deactivated her account. That night I went back to the hotel room. She didn't call. I didn't call. I drifted off to sleep.

I woke up at 04:30. I decided the commandant's comments weren't enough. I felt he was pandering to the backlash. His words were hollow. They lacked any action. I made another post. This post is still on my social media. It stated:

> First, I am as good as can be expected. My followers experienced a rollercoaster of emotions with me this last week. All of your stories were comforting. The empathy shown revived my belief in humanity and Americans. I hope, when faced with perceived injustices, all Americans make the decision to always fight. I believe warriors never quit. I know I will never quit. This situation, like all others before it, will only make me (us) stronger. Second, I want to clarify the purpose of this whole endeavor: accountability. Without accountability, Marines (Americans) cannot heal, and the Marine Corps (America) cannot evolve as an organization. I must acknowledge that the rage escalated in my body very quickly, and perhaps my emotions didn't always provide the rational clarity the situation required. But maybe...every once in a while...a little rage is required too.

> Going forward at this point on my life's path, I must remain committed to forcing accountability across our senior leaders. I do not trust that reviews done by panels at the political/military level will bring the change we seek. And I do not trust

that it will change unless a strong enough force is applied to the system. Major changes are needed. The system needs to be broken and rebuilt. We need fresh blood and perspective across the entire system. Here's a crazy idea to illustrate my point... what if we allowed the next EWS honor graduate to become the next Commandant? If you say it's not possible for a young, intelligent, charismatic leader to lead an organization such as the Marine Corps, then I'd say you haven't been reviewing the history books you tell us to read. If you say it's not possible because that young officer can't navigate the political landscape of DC...then I'd say you're making the point for me. It's time for a new generation to assume American power. We are ready, and we reject the current system. Third, this entire experience has illustrated to me just how hungry Americans are for honesty, accountability, and reform across the government. This was expressed to me from ALL political parties. We the people want change. We the people WILL take it. We the people are ALL Americans. Follow me, and we will bring the whole fucking system down...in a constitutional manner with one loud voice. NF3

NF3 was another chess move. Knight out. Develop the midpieces. Following this post, I drove into work and sat in my temporary office. I stared at the wall for hours. I wasn't sure where this was going. Did I have a plan?

CHAPTER 13:

THE LABOR FORCE IS AMERICA—
LABOR DAY WEEKEND. THIRD VIDEO. DIVORCE.

"There is no fear in love. But perfect love drives out fear because fear has to do with punishment. The one who fears is not made in perfect love."

—John 4:18

I finally called my wife on Friday September 3, five days after she asked me to leave the house. She was upset. She pointed out that I hadn't taken her call on Wednesday and then had posted about how much I missed her on Thursday. I apologized, admitted she was right, and acknowledged I could have handled the situation better. My apology didn't alleviate her anger. She asked if we could sell the house. She wanted to move the kids back to her parents in Virginia Beach. She wanted the next six months to figure out if we should remain married. When we got off the phone, I was taken aback by how quickly she defaulted to divorce. We had never discussed divorce before. Following our phone conversation, that night I shot her an email devoid of emotion. I stated how I wanted to remain married but acknowledged it wasn't

171

completely my decision; it takes two people to make a marriage work. My only request was a timely decision on her part. I didn't want to spend the next six months while she waffled about our marriage. If she decided she wanted out, I outlined how we could split our assets. I tried to be more than fair so she could comfortably exit the marriage if that's what she wanted. She said she appreciated the email but still wanted at least an extra week to make her decision. She was bringing the kids back to the house on Sunday and still wanted me out when she arrived. We decided to meet at the house Monday, September 13, to discuss the future of our marriage.

Since my wife wasn't coming back until Sunday, I checked out of the motel and went back to the house. The media reporters were gone at this point. When I got back to the house, I noticed most of the fish were dead. It was a morbid version of the *Jerry Maguire* scene where a man in midlife crisis stares at fish. I fed the few living fish and scooped up their dead counterparts. I was glad my friend Jeff had watched our turtles. I walked up the stairs and laid in the bed. I thought coming home would make me feel better, but I quickly realized sitting in the big empty house with only memories of my family made it worse. I immediately started getting depressed. Then my phone rang.

The phone call was from Eddie Gallagher, whose reputation preceded him. Eddie was a Navy SEAL prosecuted by the United States Navy for allegedly killing an ISIS prisoner. He was acquitted of all murder charges while I was at MARSOC. His trial was the talk of the town back then. Eddie was a person who experienced the inequities of the military's legal system. My number was passed on to him from an intermediate friend. I was excited to speak with him. My first conversation with Eddie remained mostly on a human level. He listened while I vented about my contempt for senior leaders. He listened while I confessed all my personal problems.

"Stu, do you have a lawyer?"

"No. I'm thinking about representing myself."

"That's fucking stupid. You need a lawyer. I'm going to put you in contact with my guy Brian. Talk to him. You don't have to use him, but you need to get a lawyer. Also, how do you plan on raising money?"

"I'm not raising money."

"You don't have a choice. Situations like these require lawyers, experts, relocation expenses, etc. You must raise money. I have a foundation with my wife called the Pipe Hitter Foundation. Get on a call with my wife and me tomorrow to discuss more about partnering with a nonprofit."

When I got off the phone with Eddie, his lawyer Brian called me within ten minutes. Brian was a JAG (Judge Advocate Generals Corps lawyer) Air Force lieutenant colonel in the Reserves. He developed a relationship with Eddie while representing other defendants during Eddie's trial. Brian is independently wealthy, intelligent, and gay. I liked him immediately. Brian told me he loved my first video but my second video scared him. He said he couldn't even watch it. I laughed. I explained why I was so upset with the general officers in the military. I outlined my perceived mistreatment: fired without an investigation, attacked about my mental health, and relegated to an office within eyeshot of the commanding officer.

He took a deep breath and said, "You'll get your chance to say everything you're telling me. And what's great is that it has the added benefit of being true."

When I got off the phone with Brian, my anxiety subsided enough to drift off to sleep.

When I woke up the next morning, I took the call with Eddie and his wife, Andrea. Andrea ran point on the conversation. She explained how the government raided her house at gunpoint while she was in the kitchen with their children. It was clear where her passion for helping service members originated. She explained how she engaged the media while Eddie was in jail. She asked me if Jackie was comfortable speaking to the media. I laughed and then explained our complicated situation. Andrea asked whether Jackie could call her. After speaking with them for an hour, partnering with their nonprofit was a no-brainer. I texted Andrea's phone number to Jackie after the call and pleaded with Jackie to call her. I promised Jackie it would make her feel better.

Many people in the aftermath questioned my partnership with the Gallaghers. Their name brand and organization were polarizing in many circles. But despite the criticism of the Gallaghers, I found them both to be very compassionate and genuinely eager to help. However, their method for addressing the conflict was not always in sync with my vision. This seam created larger issues later.

The next morning, Sunday September 5, my dad called as I left the house and headed back to the motel. I revealed that Jackie and I were going through a tough time and that I was driving to a motel. He owned a vacation rental in Emerald Isle, North Carolina. As if he already knew I was having marriage problems, he told me the condo would be available starting the next day, Monday, until I got back on my feet. I thanked him. I didn't want to spend much more time in my motel.

When I got into my motel room, I stared at the ceiling. I thought about Labor Day and the significance of the holiday in America. I thought about General Mattis and his board member positions with General Dynamics. I thought about General Austin and his board member positions with Raytheon. They were exactly the opposite of Labor Day in my opinion. I decided to make another post:

> Tomorrow is Labor Day. The day we celebrate the hard hat wearing, timecard punching, hungover but still gets up and goes to work hero. And I just couldn't resist the opportunity to celebrate that hero with some sentiments that I think belong to the entire Labor Force. The Labor Force has this to say to the American

Government...perhaps, we the people are not as divided as you want US to be. We understand that divisions make it easier to control US. We understand that divisions can be exploited. Fox News and CNN clearly illustrate our point. We have to watch both commentaries to understand how one side is spinning a story towards the other side. What if we just had an organization that reported the facts. We could come up with a name for it...like the news. We the people are not black/white, straight/gay, Christian/atheist, mask/nomask, police/community, wallstreet/mainstreet...so on and so on. We are Americans. Adjectives are not required. The Labor Force seeks fundamental change in our Government. We reject your system. If you're not paying attention, you fucking should be. Refer to the Declaration of Independence as a reminder. "Governments are instituted among men, deriving their just powers from the consent of the governed. That whenever any form of Government becomes destructive of these ends, it is the Right of the People to alter or to abolish it, and to institute new Government, laying its foundation on such principles and organizing its powers in such form, as to them shall seem most likely to affect their safety and happiness.... When a long train of abuses and usurpations, pursuing invariably the same object evinces a design to reduce them under absolute despotism, it is their right, it is their duty, to throw off such Government, and to provide new guards for their future security." Second, the Labor Force wants to make another statement to the military establishment. Our current National Security Establishment created after World War II does not work. We the people seek fundamental change.

President Eisenhower, a man with more experience/insight than any other American past or present on this matter, clearly anticipated our current problems with this quote, "In the councils of government, we must guard against the acquisition of unwarranted influence, whether sought or unsought, by the military-industrial complex. The potential for the disastrous rise of misplaced power exists and will persist. We must never let the weight of this combination endanger our liberties or democratic process. We should take nothing for granted. Only an alert and knowledgeable citizenry can compel the proper meshing of the huge industrial and military machinery of defense with our peaceful methods and goals, so that security and liberty may prosper together." How many General Officers and high ranking OSD employees get jobs with Lockheed Martin, Boeing, General Dynamics, Raytheon, Haliburton, or Northrop Grumman. I dare you to publish that stat. Do you think we're stupid? We can't ALL be wrong. They only have the power because we allow it. Every generation needs a revolution. e3

My new lawyer Brian called me after I made the Labor Day post. He scolded me for making another post. "You need to stop posting. I'm can't deescalate the situation if you keep antagonizing them. You need to trust me." His statement on the surface made a lot of sense, but I was always hesitant when someone told me to trust them.

That week I moved into my dad's vacation rental. Needing some more personal belongings, while Jackie and the kids were away at school, I snuck into the house. When I walked in, I froze at the sight of boxes all over the house. Jackie was packing everyone's belongings. She had already made her decision to move forward with the divorce. Now I had to wait until Monday for her to tell me face-to-face. Realizing that I would probably be in the condo longer than I anticipated, I grabbed even more clothes, a handful of books, and some other personal items for my condo.

That Friday, September 10, now living in my dad's vacation rental, I made a third video heading into the September 11 weekend. The third video addressed an emotional aspect of war that I thought had links to the problems in the American government. I felt a service member questioning leadership's approach to war was logical. I didn't think asking senior leaders for accountability was crazy. But following the video, I was painted as even crazier than before. The relevant quotes from the third video are below:

> Hey everybody, Stu Scheller. I wanted to make a video for all the people who have supported me and been with me for the last two weeks.... I wanted to also apologize to Brian my lawyer who has worked very hard going back and forth with the Marine Corps to get me out.... But I feel like with the path I'm on, I'm just trying to listen to the voice inside me and do what I think is right.... And specifically going into 9/11 there was some things that I wanted to say. But to re-cap, I just asked for accountability in my first video. Accountability from my senior leaders. And I still haven't received that. But after I made that video, I felt like the organization that I loved and the people that I trusted the most turned their backs on me and I was filled with rage, and so I

made the second video. And I still stand by everything I said in that video, but I was angry, and I
acknowledge that. But it felt like everyone wanted
to attack me with projecting PTSD, or saying that
I was having a breakdown, or that I was suicidal.
I had to get mental health evaluations, because I
felt like that was easier for them to understand
than me be principled in my stance.

At this point in the video, I tell a war story from when I
watched a Taliban fighter lie on a grenade in his dying moment.
The purpose of the story was an illustration of respect among enemies in war. I was trying to communicate that war doesn't have
good and bad guys. Only people with different perspectives. Perspectives informed by ideas. I was trying to explain that in our
current construct, the nation-state monopolized utilization of violence is a source of power that should not be taken for granted
by senior leaders. This perceived power is given to the government
voluntarily by the people. But I didn't clearly make the connection
in the video. From the war story, I go on to talk about my understanding of emotions and how they drive actions in war:

> The opposite of love is not hate. It's fear. On
> 9/11 twenty years ago America came together
> based on fear. And we did things based on fear.
> There are ways to do things based on rational
> thinking and unity that don't involve fear. And
> part of it starts with respecting different opinions
> in all people. Even if you don't agree with them…
> love is not absent from war.

This logic still permeates American culture. Most wars start by
stirring the fear of the American people rather than focusing on the
love for those we want to protect. I concluded the video by saying:

General officers for the last twenty years have given bad advice. Consistently. And none of them have been held accountable…. The people in the establishment right now currently have the power because we allow it to happen. There is change upon us. I love and respect all people with different opinions. I possess the ability to inflict violence. I am asking for accountability of my senior leaders. I love the Constitution. I love America. I love Americans. I love my family. And I believe in myself. And I believe in a higher power. Maybe on 9/11 twenty years later, we as a nation can come together based on mutual respect and love, and then once we do that, there is no stopping us.

Two sentences were ripped from this video and criminalized: "I possess the ability to inflict violence. I am asking for accountability of my senior leaders." Both sentences were factually true. But the government felt it constituted a threat.

It is also relevant to note that I had three books on my table when I made the video. The three books in the video were three of the five books I grabbed when I stopped by my house earlier in the week. *On War* by Clausewitz, *The Complete Works of Aristotle*, and *Imperium* by Francis Yockey. I bought *Imperium* years ago at a bookstore because the subtitle was "The Philosophy and History of Politics." I flipped through and read a couple of pages, and it captured my attention. It seemed like a book worth reading, so I bought it. I did not research the author in the bookstore when I purchased the book. It turns out that Francis Yockey was a fascist. This was also used against me.

Brian called me after the third video and told me Major General Alford's lawyer was upset that I had made another video. The Marine Corps assumed that since I now had a lawyer I would remain silent. When they realized my lawyer may not have control, the dialogue between the lawyers started getting adversarial. Brian talked to me about it, "I think you may not be listening to me because you don't fully trust me yet. Let me be clear, Stu, if you were my little brother, I'd tell you to stop. You're only making it worse for yourself. I can get you a deal this week, but you have to remain quiet. If you continue making statements, they are going to throw you in jail. I saw what they did against Eddie Gallagher. The government doesn't play fair when they are upset."

"I appreciate that, Brian. But now let me be clear, I'm not your little brother. You have no idea what I've been through. You're here to provide advice. I'll decide what to do based on that advice." When we got off the phone it was a little tense, but we softened the tension with funny memes to each other the rest of the week.

That Monday I stopped by the house to speak with my wife. She had put away all the boxes anticipating my visit. After the kids finished dinner, she and I sat at the table to discuss if she wanted to remain in the marriage. She had written out multiple pages of notes. I let her get through the first page and then grew impatient. All I could think about were all the boxes. "Babe, I'm happy to listen to all of this, but I need you to cut to the chase. Do you want to remain married, or do you want to get a divorce?"

"I want out," she said.

"Why?" I demanded.

"I spoke to Andrea from the Pipe Hitter Foundation last week. She said you would be fine if you didn't make any more social media posts. But my friends told me you posted a third video."

"I did. Did you watch it?"

"No. I just can't believe you're still making posts."

"Jackie, that's not a reason for divorce if you haven't even listened to the content. I will play the video for you right now."

"I don't want to watch it. I just want to learn to play golf in retirement. You want to fundamentally change the government. I think we are on separate paths."

"Would you like to go to counseling?"

"I think it would be best if we were just friends, and we have a positive relationship moving forward."

I started tearing up. "OK. I can't listen to the rest of your notes. Thanks for being direct with me. We can talk division of the assets another time. I have to go." Then I walked out of the house.

The following day, Tuesday afternoon, Brian bartered a legal deal with the Marine Corps. I could have resolution to the situation if I was willing to take the deal. But I wasn't sure I wanted the deal. They were offering me a deal, and the investigation still hadn't been provided to me. They wanted me to accept a deal without having all the facts. But more than that, still not a single officer had addressed the content of my statements. They were very quick to hold me accountable, which added to my frustration that they were absolved of the same principles of accountability.

I could sense that my message of accountability had drifted off track. I concluded that I needed to be more specific with my demands for accountability. I needed to identify a person. General Mark A. Milley, the chairman of the Joint Chiefs, was the easiest target. At that time it became public knowledge that he had usurped the power of President Trump because he disagreed with Trump's political views. Milley, through a long string of questionable comments and behavior, made it very easy for the American people to dislike him. But unfortunately, he wasn't accountable for the disaster in Afghanistan. The chain of command for Afghanistan went from President Biden, to Secretary of Defense Austin, and then to General McKenzie as the combatant commander. The focus of my accountability endeavor had to be General McKenzie. He is the one who should have convinced the president from a professional military perspective.

I started reading the *Manual for Courts-Martial and the Uniform Code of Military Justice*. I wondered, *Was there a way I could bring charges against General McKenzie if no other officer had the courage?* I found it in Rule 307 of the *Manual for Courts-Martial*: preferral of charges.

CHAPTER 14:

ACCOUNTABILITY IS A TWO-WAY STREET— FOURTH VIDEO. GENERAL AWAKENING. GAG ORDER.

"All institutions of government learn, adapt, and make appropriate changes. This is even more imperative for the national security agencies and personnel, where the stakes are high…. Fortunately, in time American democracy will make those adaptations. The question will be at what price and how quickly."[3]

—Gabriel Marcella, "Understanding the Interagency Process: The Challenge of Adaptation," *Affairs of State: The Interagency and National Security*

I still went into work every day the week of September 13–17. The tension was high. The enlisted Marines continued celebrating me. The officers continued giving me dirty looks. Colonel Emmel still wouldn't approve my leave. I tried chipping away at medical appointments and other out-processing events outside the office. My resignation at this point stagnated for weeks at Marine Corps headquarters. The Marine Corps could have accepted my resignation and allowed me to exit the service, but they, too, wanted accountability. They were holding my resignation until my legal situation was adjudicated.

A legal deal was offered to me on Tuesday, September 14. The deal was nonjudicial punishment contingent on me resigning, giving up retirement, and accepting a general discharge. I told them I needed to think about it. At that point, I still hadn't met face-to-face with my lawyer, Brian. Wanting me to have human lawyer interaction, Brian convinced me to also use Major Brummond, the military lawyer I threw out of my office weeks back. Following his advice, I set up an appointment at Tyler's office on Wednesday to make the peace. I asked about the investigation, and Tyler informed me he hadn't seen it. So, I asked Tyler, "Have you ever seen a legal deal offered by a general without an investigation?"

"No," he said. "This situation is definitely one of a kind. I think they want closure quickly." I left his office that day with a million thoughts, and then I realized I hadn't asked about my desire to prefer charges against General McKenzie. I texted Tyler once I got home: "Hey, I need a JAG officer. Not you. Willing to swear in an official statement/charge I plan on delivering tomorrow. Please advise on a time."

"Sorry I can't do that for a number of reasons. I further advise you not to pursue this idea of preferring charges against a senior commander as it will only cause you prejudice and potential legal harm. Give me a call if you have any questions or if you intend pursuing this any further."

His text reminded me why the entire legal system was flawed. The senior defense attorney on the East Coast for the Marine Corps was advising me to back away from pursuing legal action against a senior military officer because it might end badly for me. Obviously, he wasn't paying attention and didn't know me very well.

Thursday morning, before work and school, I showed up to the house to tell the kids Jackie and I were going through a divorce.

The entire family got on the couch for another family meeting. There is no easy way to break that news. I kept it short, "Your mom and I have disagreements about how we want to live our lives going forward. We are getting divorced. You are going to move up to Virginia Beach and live with your mom." The kids processed the information. There were some emotions, but after five minutes of hugs everyone seemed to be all right. Then the kids went back to playing the Nintendo Switch as if nothing had happened. I nodded to Jackie and walked back out of the house.

By that afternoon, the Marine Corps grew impatient that I hadn't accepted their offered deal. General Alford's lawyer warned us that I had until the end of the day on Friday to accept or reject the deal. But I knew all along that I had more to say. The entire week I delayed responding to the deal until I was ready to make another statement. I wanted to bring the message back to accountability. I was going to target General McKenzie in my demand for accountability. That Thursday night, I put on my khaki service uniform and made a fourth video. I needed maximum effect. I introduced myself, then stated:

> I've been advised through the legal channels that continued challenges to my military and political leadership could result in pre-trial confinement and/or escalation of my legal situation which I'll get into. But I thought this message, being the culmination of everything I've put together up to this point, was important.... To recap my position, in the fall out of Afghanistan I demanded accountability of my senior leaders. I stated then I understood that I might lose my battalion commander seat, my retirement, and my family stability. As it has played out, I have in fact lost all three of those things. Would I do it again? I don't know. But I can explain to you why I made that decision. Look-

ing at the military and political establishment of the American government, I was seeing key leaders who weren't being held accountable. They were abusing their positions of power at the expense of the everyday American. And everything I've fought for is counter to that. The future that my sons are going to grow up in is contingent upon the organization being able to evolve which only happens through accountability.

I then provided an update on the legal deal offered by the Marine Corps. I acknowledged the video would most likely invalidate the offer, but I understood that and still chose to make the statement. Then I continued:

> Believe it or not I don't want to start controversy. I didn't make it seventeen years in the Marine Corps, and become a battalion commander, by saying whatever I wanted, whenever I wanted. But as I sat here and thought about the changes that needed to take place in our key organizations, I just didn't see anyone else speaking up.

I then chastised the retired generals who wrote a letter demanding resignations from the active generals. I knew the retired generals' tactic was ineffective if they remained hidden and beholden to their retirement. Their actions weren't enough. I continued with the video:

> I think our lack of accountability may come from the post-Vietnam generation who now shows respect to service members at the expense of offering criticism. Criticism that I think our general officers need. I think history demonstrates general officers don't always have the right answer.

I then spoke directly to General Berger and reminded him that his tactical pivot of the force was meaningless if he couldn't hold senior leaders accountable. I then reminded him of General Amos's reawakening. I finished the video by pointing out that:

> [General Amos] said the role of the commandant was to protect the very soul of the Marine Corps. But he focused on the NCOs. The NCOs that in my opinion have fought bravely and valiantly for the last twenty years. I do believe there is an awakening that needs to take place, but it's not at the NCO level, it's at the general officer level. The people who are not being held accountable. The people who are leading this organization. And I ask that you use your leadership, provide introspection, and identify the problems.

Then I pivoted the conversation to my target of the video, General McKenzie:

> General McKenzie, sir. You made comments that are public record on August 31. You stated you made bad assumptions, left hundreds of Americans in Afghanistan, and itemized equipment left behind equaling hundreds of millions of dollars. I know you are a great American. I know you didn't intend to fail. I know you have served very honorably and are probably a great leader. But that doesn't absolve you from the accountability of your bad assumptions.

I then described my plan for preferring charges against General McKenzie. I also talked about the Pipe Hitter Foundation Fund established on my behalf for legal fees. I ended by saying:

I love America, I love the Constitution, I love Americans. But we can't all be wrong. You only have the power because we allow it. My name is Lieutenant Colonel Stuart Scheller, and I was the only officer in the entire American coalition fired in the debacle of the Afghanistan fallout. I acknowledge that I should have been fired. However, the hypocrisy of the general officers not being held to the same standard is a microcosm for the entire problem that's bringing down the institutions of the great Republic that we love. I implore you, please use some introspection and fix these problems.

Following the video, I also posted Tyler's text conversation warning me not to prefer charges. I also posted the charge sheet I intended to use in my preferral of charges against General McKenzie. Expectedly, as soon the posts hit, a new wave of comments, texts, and phone calls came pouring in. Brian called within an hour of the posts. He didn't seem as upset as he was after the third video. "Well, I guess you didn't want to take the offer," he said laughing.

"Call them tomorrow and figure out if the offer is still valid," I said. "If not, let's see where this goes. Can you send me the paperwork for preferral of charges? I'd like to submit them to Colonel Emmel tomorrow."

When I went into work the next day, Friday, September 17, I didn't know what to expect. My commanding officer happened to be in Quantico that day. When I walked in, my executive officer, Lieutenant Colonel Mannochio, told me Colonel Emmel wanted a conference call with the three of us. When we got on the phone, Colonel Emmel scolded me for posting another video. "I can't believe I have to deal with this from a lieutenant colonel. Up to this point, I've continued to warn you about the Marine Corps social media policy, and you've continued to make posts. It stops today.

On the desk, you will see a printed-out copy of a gag order. I want you to read it while I'm on the phone and then ask any questions."

The gag order stated:

> You clearly stated that you seek complete dismantling of the current system of government in the United States; you explicitly reject the ideas of working through established political process to achieve systemic change. You have called upon Americans to be willing to inflict violence in pursuit of your ideals…. As such, you have proven unwilling to conform to the laws and regulations that govern our conduct as Marines. You have flatly refused to respect the boundaries of constitutionally protected speech delineated for military officers…. Accordingly, effective immediately upon your receipt below, you are hereby ordered to refrain from posting any and all material, in any form and without exception, to any social media. In this context, the term "social media" shall be construed very broadly to include any medium by which you may share information with groups of people. It includes more traditional form of social media (e.g., Facebook, YouTube, LinkedIn) as well as nontraditional methods one might use to circumvent established social media (e.g., mass emails, group text messages, electronic bulletin boards). You are also prohibited from communicating through third parties or proxies. This order is addressed to you as a corrective measure so that additional measures are not necessitated in accordance with the manual for courts martial. The duration is indefinite, and it applies until explicitly rescinded in writing by me.

I was first put off after reading the gag order. I felt I had clarified the controversial, "Bring the whole f'ing system down" comment with my follow-up post: "Bring the whole f'ing system down in a constitutional manner with one loud voice." But I guess Colonel Emmel, like many others, didn't read the follow-up post. And yes, I guess it was true that in my third video I did say "I possess the ability to commit violence." But I felt like he ripped that one comment from all the other context. He didn't mention the multiple times I talked about love in that video or understanding and respecting other people's opinions. Colonel Emmel interpreted it as, "explicitly reject the ideas of working through established political process to achieve systemic change. You have called upon Americans to be willing to inflict violence in pursuit of your ideals." Did he really believe that, or was he trying to justify a potential overreach of his authority as a commander? Could he really prevent me from communicating through third parties? Could he really implement this order indefinitely?

I thought about not signing the document. As if Colonel Emmel could sense my delay over the phone, he spoke up. "It doesn't matter if you don't sign. This gag order applies to you time now. If you refuse to sign, we will just write in 'refused to sign' and then we will issue you another formal counseling for refusing an order. If you violate the gag order leaving this office, you will be held accountable."

I signed the document but had more to say. "Sir, I sent you an email with the preferral of charges for General McKenzie. All I need for you to do is administer the oath so that I send the charge sheet up to General Alford. We can do that over the phone."

"Stu, I'm not going to do that over the phone. We can talk about it when I get back on Monday." I walked out of his office and pretended to work on the computer the rest of the day.

When I got home that night, I read an article from the publication *Task and Purpose*, an online magazine specializing in military news. It is owned by North Equity Venture Capital. Zach Iscol owns North Equity. Zach Iscol was a former Marine who comes from "family money" in New York. He ran for New York City mayor on the Democratic ticket. Zach is a big political donor to the Democratic Party, and his ties to Hillary Clinton can be found with a quick Google search. Jeffery Schogol is Zach's senior Pentagon reporter at *Task and Purpose*. Jeff started writing articles about me after the release of my fourth video. The headline of his first article read "This Marine officer wants to charge a general with 'dereliction of duty' over Afghanistan. He Can't. Good initiative, bad judgment." *Task and Purpose* first released the article on September 18. In the initial version of the article, Schogol quoted a former JAG officer turned university professor who said, "I haven't read the manual for court martial recently, but I remember that junior officers can't prefer charges against a senior officer." Ten days after the release of the article, on September 27, Schogol was forced to fact-check and update the article. He took out "He Can't" from the title and dropped the quote from the former JAG. In other words, ten days after the article, Schogol took the time to fact-check his article, realized I was right, and was forced to quietly update the article. When he updated the article, he did not explain how or why he updated the article. The practice is borderline criminal in my opinion—certainly journalistically disingenuous and intentionally misleading. But at that point I hadn't realized how far *Task and Purpose* was willing to go to discredit me.

Following the *Task and Purpose* article I started reviewing articles about me with more scrutiny. Many of them seemed to paint me as right-wing extremist. They claimed I only demanded accountability because a Democrat was the president. Others preferred to call me a violent extremist. Others said it was about the money. In the comments section of the articles people were saying things like, "He might be schizophrenic. He's the appropriate age." "He's a threat to our way of life." "He's another suffering veteran that's going to end up homeless." "This is all a ploy to run for political office. See you in '22." I slammed my computer shut.

Reading media-spun narratives while legally unable to speak was a painful experience. *I'm not going to let them define me*, I thought. *I'm stronger than all these people realize.*

That weekend, only days after my fourth video, General McKenzie held a press conference about a drone strike he approved on August 29 in response to the preventable attack at the Kabul airfield. He stated the strike did not kill any combatants as he and the president had originally reported, that he now understood those killed consisted of only seven children and three adults. "It was a mistake and I offer my sincere apology. As the combatant commander I am fully responsible for this strike and its tragic outcome."

This has got to be enough for him to be held accountable, I thought to myself. *At this point, there is no way my chain of command won't allow me to prefer charges. What else does it take for senior leaders to admit failure and hold one of their own accountable?*

The next Monday, September 20, I came into work eager to submit my charges on General McKenzie. I sat down with Colonel Emmel and had a conversation. "Sir, did you read the email I sent you? I have all the proper paperwork filled out. All I need you to do is administer the oath so that I can send the charge sheet up to General Alford."

"Stu, you don't understand how this works. You cannot prefer charges against a senior ranking officer."

"Sir, we can pull out the *Manual for Courts-Martial*. It clearly states it in rule 307. You can't prevent me from what is my legal right."

"You do not have this right. I'll read what you think has happened, I'll evaluate the situation, and then I'll determine if a charge sheet is required."

"Well, sir, I disagree. But if you won't let me submit my charges, can you at least give me feedback if you decide to submit the charges?"

"No. You do not rate feedback on my decisions."

I walked out of the office obviously frustrated. I called my lawyer.

Brian's advice was, "Don't you do anything crazy, Stu. The general's lawyer doesn't understand the difference between referral and preferral either. I'll handle this at their level. You just sit tight."

"But Colonel Emmel said I didn't deserve feedback. Is there a way I can compel him to give me feedback?"

"There is. You can fill out a request redress form outlining your complaint. He has a time limit to formally respond, or it gets routed up to the secretary of the Navy. And one other thing, they rescinded your offer after your fourth video."

"So, what does that mean?"

"It means we continue to wait until we figure out what they are going to do."

I sat down in my temporary office frustrated. General McKenzie by his own admission left hundreds of Americans and hundreds of millions of dollars of equipment in Afghanistan. Some of the gear may have been left regardless, but some of it was obviously left based on our poor planning and hasty exit. It was hard not to think about the year I spent at Infantry Training Battalion as a captain going to bed every night plagued with anxiety for losing five machine gun optics. I focused my frustration by looking up the request redress form. I quickly filled it out. Without talking to Brian, I shot the form to Colonel Emmel. In the text of the email I said, "Sir you told me today that I cannot prefer charges. You said you would not administer the oath. You said I can only advise. You said you would determine wrongdoing. You said I didn't deserve any feedback on your thought process. I think everything in those comments is wrong and illegal. See attached." I cc'd Brian.

Brian immediately called me. "Stu, I can't work like this. I told you not to do anything. I was working it at my level, and you just marginalized our credibility. Now they will get entrenched in their position. And the sarcastic tone in the text of your email is not helpful. That's the type of stuff that will make us lose at appeal. We are supposed to be a team, and you are not doing things as a team member."

I was still upset. "Brian, being on a team means everyone wins and loses together. I'm the only one with anything to lose here. This is not a team."

"I'm trying to help you, but again, I can't work like this. If you want my help, you need to communicate with me before you post, email, or text your chain of command."

"I understand. I apologize," I said. I hung up and went back to the old house. Jackie had asked me to stop by so that we could move the fish tank into the garage. She was staging the house, as we planned on listing it that weekend. The fish were all dead at this point. Jeff had returned the turtles, but they were relegated to a baby pool in the garage while we moved the fish tank.

"What are you going to do with the turtles?" I asked.

"Do you want them? I can't bring them to Virginia Beach."

"I can't take care of myself right now. No, I don't want the turtles."

"OK, well I'll find a pond close by, and we'll let them go."

I finished moving the aquarium, still upset at my boss, now saddened at the fate of my pet turtles, and Jackie then handed me a separation agreement. "What the fuck is this? How did you already speak to a lawyer and get a separation agreement? How is this possible? Why didn't we talk it through and just go to an arbitrator?"

"She works for both of us."

"No, Jackie. When a lawyer draws up a contract for you, she doesn't work for both of us. She didn't even talk to me."

"Look, all it says are the things in your email. Please just take a look and let me know what you think."

I stormed out of the house. I sent the separation agreement back that night. It was nowhere near what I had stipulated in the agreement. And I didn't have the mental capacity to review any more legal documents. I told her we could revisit the document later. She was understanding. She thanked me for moving the fish tank and reminded me that I needed to sign some forms so that we could list the house that weekend.

The following day, Tuesday, September 21, the Pipe Hitter Foundation launched the donation portal. The initial week of the campaign, after I released my final video, the donation fund shot up to $75,000. *So awesome*, I thought, *that is enough to cover my legal expenses and Jackie's relocation expenses. That in addition to our savings and the money we make from selling the house will tide us over until I can get another job.*

The week wound down without incident. As we entered the weekend, I remained in purgatory. At that point my investigation wasn't complete, there was no offer on the table, no formal charges had been levied against me, my resignation was not being accepted, I wasn't permitted to take leave, and I wasn't allowed to prefer charges. *Was I done?* I wondered. *Would any senior officer address the content of my statements?* I knew the following week, on Tuesday, September 28, and Wednesday September 29, Secretary of Defense Lloyd Austin, Chairman of the Joint Chiefs General Milley, and CENTCOM Combatant Commander General McKenzie were testifying to the Senate and House Armed Forces Committees. *Would Congress be able to hold the generals accountable?* I wondered. I also knew the FY 2022 Defense Department budget was moving through the House of Representatives. At that point, the defense budget had not made it to the Senate. I believed Congress's best leverage over the defense department was the budget. Other authorities or threats wouldn't be sufficient. And it was perfect timing, the budget was up for review at the exact time the congressional testimony took place.

I read the *Manual for Courts-Martial* again. Rule 305 defines pretrial confinement. It states, "Confinement is necessary because it is foreseeable that the confine will not appear at trial, pretrial hearing, or preliminary hearing, or the confine will engage in serious criminal misconduct and less severe forms of restraint are inadequate."

Did I meet this threshold? I wondered. They definitely couldn't argue I was flight risk. I had been to work every day since my first video even after they denied my leave request. I guess they would need to argue that my conduct is "serious criminal misconduct and less severe forms of restraint are inadequate." It still seemed like a stretch. I decided to break the gag order. I wanted to test their legal theories and bring more attention to the hypocrisy of the system prior to the general's testimony.

CHAPTER 15:

ARE ALL PEOPLE IN JAIL BAD?—
FINAL POST. JAIL. COLD SHOWERS.

*"In short, maneuver warfare is a philosophy for gen-
erating the greatest decisive effect against the enemy
at the least possible cost to ourselves—a philosophy for
'fighting smart.'"*

—A captain who never experienced combat yet
wrote MCDP-1

Saturday, September 25, I made another post with multiple pur-
poses. First, I wanted to see if my command would justify sending me to jail for violating a gag order. Second, I wanted to separate
myself from political parties and demonstrate how my contempt
was with the entire system of government and not one political
party. Third, I wanted to apply pressure on the generals testifying
before Congress. And fourth, I felt publicity would be good for
fundraising. Because of the divisive nature of the post, months later I deleted it. But it hung on my social media for months and was
quoted by many news outlets. It's still easy to find on the internet.
Below are relevant quotes from the post:

WE don't want our children abused in the same failed systems. The systems remain, despite their repeated failures, because key holding hypocrites have safe haven within the system.... The keyholders refuse to take accountability when it is so obvious. They are unable or unwilling to do what is right. But WE are not like the Apathetic American. WE have faith. WE believe what you stand for can only be defined by what you're willing to risk. They need US scared. They need US silenced. They need US divided. Fear, division, and ignorance facilitates control. WE the people are not republican/democrat, black/white, straight/gay, Christian/atheist, mask/nomask, police/community, wallstreet/mainstreet, so on and so on. We are Americans. Adjectives are not required. Don't dim your light to walk into their darkness. Walk into their darkness and light shit up.

After this opening statement, I proceeded to light shit up.

President Trump. I was told by everyone to kiss the ring because of your following and power. I refuse. While I respect your foreign policy positions...you do not have the ability to pull US together.... President Obama. Great at speeches obviously weak in any intestinal fortitude. President Bush Jr. Great at speeches obviously ignorant in thinking he could export democracy. President Clinton. Great at bringing Congress together, obviously morally bankrupt. This includes his wife.

I then went on to refer to General Mattis. I referenced the time he visited when I was a lieutenant, and it appeared to me his female companion was a prop. I told him he appeared fake and dishonest. "For all your talk about the 5-3-5 and counterinsurgency, can we go back and review the record? The academics loved you. You talked about reading books all the time. The only problem was you didn't win any wars. Maybe you should have read different books." I also attack Generals Petraeus and Flynn in the same manner. They all demonstrated dishonesty at one point.

I then shifted my contempt to the academics in military universities. "My contempt for the academics who have attached themselves to the military machine runs deep. I will never relate to a person who refused to fight in the arena yet feels entitled enough to offer opinions as if the lions should listen. Critics." I illustrated my point by showing how academics prevented evolution in the key manual for the Marine Corps—MCDP 1. "Maneuver Warfare is outdated. It's not attrition vs maneuver. It's decentralization vs. synchronization. And the critical question of where that balance occurs is the question you failed to address in the current version of MCDP 1. Marines all think decentralization should occur at the lowest levels despite a deeper understanding of how to maximize combat power. But I'm sure your generation of deep thinkers knew that."

I then pivoted to the actively serving general officers. I started with General Alford, the man who had recently offered and then rescinded my legal deal. I referenced a conversation we had in July. I quoted him, "We have an entire generation of LtCols who don't know how to make decisions. They feel the need to ask permission." General Alford later charged me with disrespect for that statement. Ironic that after I quoted the general about his perception that field grade officers' were indecisive, I was later charged by that same general for my decision. I also attacked my previous general, General Donovan, the man we reported Colonel Kenney's inappropriate behavior to through back channels. He refused to do anything about it. "General Donovan, thanks for finishing my fitrep multiple months late as soon as I hit the news. Is it safe to assume you processed the report when I hit the news so that you didn't look bad? It's about your optics, it's never been about US.

But if you're angry about me speaking the truth, send your regimental commander to come find me again."

I ended the post by saying, "What happens when all you do is speak truth and no one wants to hear it? But they can probably stop listening because I'm crazy, right? Colonel Emmel, please have the MPs waiting for me at 0800 on Monday. I'm ready for jail."

As soon as I finished the post, my wife called me and told me she had accepted an offer on our house. She had emailed me documents that I needed to sign to go under contract. I didn't tell her that I was probably going to jail on Monday. I made sure that I filled out all the documents and sent them back to her.

Brian called me Saturday night, "Stu, you all right?"

"No, Brian. I'm pretty fucking far from all right."

"Just know that I got your back. Don't take your phone into work. Write my number down and call me when you get to jail."

When I got off the phone with Brian I realized I needed a plan for communication with the outside world if I went to jail. I called my dad. "Hey, Dad, I'm going to send you a bunch of phone numbers to include my lawyer. If I go to jail on Monday, you'll be my one phone call, and then I'll need you to start calling people and serve as my proxy." My parents were both very supportive. They were happy to do it. Once I pushed my parents all the loose ends, I wiped my electronics of information I thought the government might try and use against me and then went to sleep.

I showed up to work Monday morning, and Colonel Emmel did in fact have the MPs waiting for me. He brought me into his office and handed me the confinement order. He justified my confinement by stating on the formal document that I was a "flight risk." I had no words. I didn't have the energy to argue anymore.

Then he did something strange. As I sat there looking defeated, he asked about my wife. The question angered me more than it should have, and I quickly found my words again.

"Sir, you listed on this confinement order that I'm a flight risk. I've come into work every single day. I even tried to take leave so that I could see my wife while we were having problems, and you wouldn't allow it. At the detriment of my family, I continued to come into work every day. Yet still somehow you justified that I'm a flight risk. And now that you're sending me to jail under false pretenses, you have the nerve to finally ask about my family." This response angered him.

"Hand me your phone and then head out with the MPs."

"Do you think I'm stupid enough to bring my phone into the office at the date and time we agreed to send me to jail?" Then I stormed out of his office and was escorted into a police car by the military police. My executive officer, Lieutenant Colonel Mannochio, escorted me and the MPs to jail in the car. On the way, I leaned over to him and said, "Mike, I'm supposed to have an inventory sheet of items that I bring with me to the brig." I knew this because as a commander I had sent multiple people to the brig myself.

"Don't worry about that," said Mike. "I talked to the brig, and they'll provide you the items."

When I was dropped off at jail (Camp Lejeune brig), it was awkward. The brig officer in charge was a warrant officer. He met me at the front entryway. As soon as Mike departed, the warrant officer admitted he didn't agree with the legality of my confinement but that he had a job to do. He said I wouldn't receive special treatment, but if I had any issues, I could route paperwork through the jail administration system, and he would personally address my complaints. Then he walked off, and I began my in-processing.

In-processing at jail consists of a thorough medical screening ensuring bumps, cuts, or bruises later claimed by prisoners as mistreatment were documented from the beginning. There was also a moment when as a male prisoner I was told to strip naked, pull my dick against my stomach, and then bend over and spreads my ass cheeks. Once this naked check was finished, the prisoner transformation was completed by my getting into a light blue jump suit. "I don't get underwear, or socks, or a T-shirt?" I asked as I put on the jump suit.

"No. You were supposed to bring those. If you didn't bring them, you don't get them." I cursed my executive officer under my breath. Ironically, as I finished my in-processing, I looked above the guard's desk, and there was a big picture of General Mattis. It was almost as if he were staring at me and laughing.

Before taking me to my cell, they allowed me one phone call. They told me because of COVID protocols, I wouldn't be allowed another phone call for a week. I needed to make sure I communicated everything within the five-minute call. But I had already prepared my dad. When I called him all I had to say was, "I'm in jail. I'll be fine. Tell my lawyer. Get in the media and tell everyone what has happened here." Then I hung up. The guard was almost in disbelief. "You had five minutes. Did you get disconnected?"

"I said everything that needed to be said. Take me to my cell."

The jail was very cognizant of my situation. All the guards and prisoners knew who I was from the beginning. The jail couldn't afford for anything to happen to me, so I was placed in a special-quarters cell. The Camp Lejeune brig consisted of two areas: a general-population area and a special-quarters area. The general-population area had about sixty prisoners that at certain times of the day could move freely around in a common lounge area. The prisoners of the special quarters were forced to stay in a solitary cell all day with three exceptions: one hour for TV, one hour for outside, and time to shower.

When I got into my cell, I immediately laid down in the bed and tried sleeping. As soon as I closed my eyes a guard banged on my cell door. "No sleeping!"

"We're not allowed to sleep in jail?" I asked.

"No. You can only sleep during the prescribed times."

"I don't have any books. What am I supposed to do in here?"

"Read your jail regulations." Then the guard walked away.

I spent the next twenty-four hours in solitude. The quiet time in many was beneficial for addressing my emotions and thoughts. I went through yoga poses and tried meditating. By Tuesday afternoon my lawyers showed up, and I had a meeting with them. The first time I met Brian face to face was in the jail. Tyler the Marine lawyer accompanied him. They told me they thought the Marine Corps would accept a resignation in lieu of trial.

"Why would they do that?" I asked. "I've been trying to resign this entire time."

"You're in jail illegally. You're not a flight risk. So, let's use it to our advantage. They have control of you while you are in jail. I don't think they want to give you a platform to speak at a trial. Let them keep you in here while your resignation goes through."

"Makes sense. But if I'm going to be in here for the next month while they process the resignation, I'm going to need you guys to bring me some books and writing pads."

"Will do. And by the way, your parents were on Tucker Carlson last night. They're going on Laura Ingram tonight. They are crushing it."

"I knew they would." Later that day Tyler dropped off a bunch of books and writing gear, and he finally provided me a copy of the completed investigation. *I'll read the investigation later*, I thought to myself. For my TV time that Tuesday, I chose to watch the news. They covered the general officers during the congressional testimony. I watched as multiple representatives asked questions about me. Lloyd Austin responded, "I'm not familiar with that case. I'll have to speak with the commandant about it." Later a commentator covering the testimony, talked about the hypocrisy of a lieutenant colonel speaking out and being placed in jail while the generals remained absolved of accountability. The other inmates in the special-quarters wing heard the commentator say it from their cells; we all started cheering. It was a weird moment. Then my one hour of TV time ended, and I went back to my cell.

I realized how awful the showers were my second night there. The water was a cold stream that required you to push a button for five seconds of water. I didn't want to stand in the cold stream, so I would push the button, get wet, and try to wash myself. But as soon as I lathered up, the water would stop. It was not a fun experience. As I finished the shower, and the guard escorted me back to my cell, I tried explaining the problem, "Have you ever experienced this shower?"

"No. I will never experience that shower because I will never end up in here. I'm a good person."

"So you think everyone that ends up in here is a bad person?"

"I think everyone who ends up in here breaks the rules."

"Is it possible your blind faith in the rules allows you to be controlled for someone else's benefit? Is it possible that you are more of a prisoner than me?"

He didn't appreciate my line of questioning. He watched me enter my cell, smirked at my situation, then walked away.

CHAPTER 16:

WITH FRIENDS LIKE THAT, WHO NEEDS ENEMIES?— INVESTIGATION. BETRAYAL. NARRATIVES.

"Cowardice asks the question is it safe? Expediency asks the question is it politic? Vanity asks the question is it popular. But conscience asks the question is it right? And there comes a time when one must take a position that is neither safe, nor politic, nor popular; but one must take it because it is right."

—Martin Luther King Jr

After remaining in jail for four days, I decided to read my command investigation on Thursday, September 30. There is relevant context for a command investigation that first needs to be clarified. Military command investigations don't pretend to be impartial. They are directed by the commanding officer to examine alleged misconduct. The investigating officer determines—based on his judgment—what information to include in the investigation. There are no obligations for an investigating officer to include information that doesn't support the narrative of the suspected criminal misconduct. There is also no obligation for the commanding

205

officer to assign an officer who even appears impartial. As such, General Alford, the convening authority of my legal case, chose a man named Colonel Gary A. McCullar. When assigned my investigation, Colonel McCullar was the engineer schoolhouse commanding officer. However, he had worked as General Alford's operations officer at Marine Corps Installations East two years before. These two officers had a special relationship. Colonel McCullar knew how to deliver a product to General Alford's expectations more efficiently than any other officer in the Marine Corps. Colonel McCullar was assigned the investigation so that he could find criminal misconduct in my behavior as justification for General Alford's quick dismissal of me as the commanding officer at Advanced Infantry Battalion.

The investigation demonstrates Colonel McCullar was laser-focused on the statement from my former battalion executive officer, Major Snelling, following our conversation about January 6, "Do you realize what would happen if an actual well-trained unit hit the Capitol building?" Colonel McCullar led every interview with "It's reported by another witness that LtCol Scheller has made comments about January 6th. Has LtCol Scheller ever spoke about January 6th, or do you know about any plans he has to overthrow the government?"

He also conveniently didn't interview any enlisted Marines who had served with me the past seventeen years. He wanted to only illustrate the field-grade officers' perspective. He selectively edited some of my posts, to include the one I sent to the commandant, and included them in my investigation so that my comments lacked content and seemed irrational. He selectively took some of my comments out of the videos and led the witnesses with selective comments soliciting negative reactions. He also included my medical records in the investigation. He did it to prove that I wasn't diagnosed with PTSD, but he didn't use any type of HIPAA banners or warnings when he included my medical records in the investigation. Thus, anyone who had access to the investigation had access to my medical records. It was criminal the way he handled the investigation. The investigation made me seem as bad as he wanted me to appear. But the blame isn't all on Colonel Mc-Cullar. Some of my "friends" went out of their way to demonize me as well. I'll directly quote my friend Lieutenant Colonel Jeff Cummings's statement. This was the man who I served with as company commander in 3/2. This was the man who I hung out with multiple times when he moved down to Camp Lejeune. This was the man who watched my turtles. This was the man texting me when I was in the motel trying to figure out my motives. This is the man who will become a general officer:

- **Colonel McCullar:** In one of my other interviews LtCol Scheller had told someone about the January 6th riots and how if it weren't a bunch of fat guys but personnel who were trained it would be different. Have you ever heard him say anything along those lines?

- **Lieutenant Colonel Cummings:** No, but in the manner in which you just said it, I could absolutely see him saying it. Without a doubt.

- **Colonel McCullar:** Has LtCol Scheller talked to you about what he wants to accomplish with his social media posts?

- **Lieutenant Colonel Cummings:** He hasn't. I have tried my damnedest to get that out of him and I can't get a thing out of him. You can get screen shots off my phone to show you.

- **Colonel McCullar:** Do you know if he has any contact with any individual or organization that wants to create a revolution or political change that could be counter to the laws of the United States Government?

- **Lieutenant Colonel Cummings:** Not direct ties but he alludes to it in his posts. But nothing to me. His OPSEC has been very good with who was once his close friends.

- **Colonel McCullar:** Were any of his views extreme?

- **Lieutenant Colonel Cummings:** No, not until the last week and a half. I don't know what switch has flipped for him. I would characterize him as shorter fused or short tempered but this behavior in the last seven days, in effect, has been over the top.

- **Colonel McCullar:** Was he saying any of this before he made the initial video?

- **Lieutenant Colonel Cummings:** No and even up through Saturday 8/21 at my house, there was nothing like this.

- **Colonel McCullar:** Do you have any insight into his future plans?

- **Lieutenant Colonel Cummings:** Anything I would offer would be speculative. My concern is that he is being manipulated by others in the media. Potentially politicians and or financial backers at some point who are using him as a mouthpiece and will be ditching him whenever they are done with him.

- **Colonel McCullar:** Have you seen any other inappropriate behavior by LtCol Scheller?

- **Lieutenant Colonel Cummings:** I have seen him short with his wife and children. I talked briefly to Colonel Emmel about this. Any event in isolation, it was never beyond a threshold that would lead you to question. I will give you an example. Two or three weeks ago, where he abruptly told his family "Pack up your stuff we are leaving" (from the beach). By itself it doesn't seem like much but when you look at the totality of how he is acting… He has already proven that he is willing to sacrifice his wife and children for any type of perceived gain in this to the point where the other night she was trying to FaceTime him with the kids and he hung up on her. Not even answering her calls. When you see posts later on that he wants her back that is all smoke and mirrors. That's him not him giving a rat's ass about his family.

- **Colonel McCullar:** Is there anything else that you deem relevant to this investigation that I need to be aware of?

- **Lieutenant Colonel Cummings:** What I'm still not sure of is if the events at the airport in Afghanistan were the impetus to these posts or if this was something brewing for a while and he was just waiting for an impetus for this kind to go down. I think that goes along the lines of your questions. Was he always like this or was he just waiting for the right time, place, pulpit and he had it as a seated commander. I'll tell you, I couldn't believe it when that command board came out. I know 10 other guys that are more qualified than him to serve in that billet. I was happy for my friend at the time, but it was wild to me.

And then as promised, Lieutenant Colonel Cummings provided screenshots of every conversation I had with him. The texts were included in the investigation because I'm assuming Colonel McCullar wanted to document Jeff's efforts to ascertain my motives. But it seemed irrelevant to the investigative process that texts explicitly stated, from friend to friend, that my whole endeavor was simply about accountability of our senior military leaders.

I won't call out all the names of the other lieutenant colonels who said similar things. Most of the other officers were probably scared for their career and decided to protect themselves. They questioned my combat record, smile, mental health, demeanor, communication skills, so on and so on. No one said anything positive. They all universally disagreed with the delivery. No one agreed with the content of the statements.

As I finished reading the investigation and paced around my cell in a homicidal rage, the prison guard stopped by and told me I had a legal visit. I followed the guard down the long hall to the visitation room. Tyler was smiling, and Brian was frowning. Almost as if Tyler could tell I had just read the investigation and needed some cheering up, he started rattling off good news, "There was a 'Free Scheller' protest/parade outside the base this morning. Also, you'll also be happy to know that your parents are showing up on television shows across the nation. And if that wasn't enough, the Pipe Hitter Foundation fund in now over $2 million."

I stared at him in disbelief. I went from the lowest of lows to the highest of highs. It was a roller coaster of emotion.

"But it's not all good news," said Brian interrupting my temporary smile. "The comments you made about President Trump are getting picked up all over the news. President Trump is angry. Eddie Gallagher spoke to him on the phone. The president said he is going speak out against you in the media. Eddie may have talked him down, but that was a mistake on your part attacking him."

"I spoke out against all the previous presidents."

"The other presidents aren't Trump. The people who donated to you are asking for their money back."

"What kind of person donates to a man who goes to jail for speaking the truth and then asks for their money back once they realize his political views don't align with theirs?"

"Lots of people. Plus you have to realize what President Trump did for Eddie. You hurt Eddie by speaking out against President Trump."

"The stated mission for Eddie's organization is to help service member in need. It doesn't say anything about me needing to agree with all his personal political feelings."

"No, of course not. But this is reality. You need to start making compromises, or you won't have any friends left. And speaking of compromises, the Marine Corps rejected our offer for a resignation in lieu of trial. They want their pound of flesh. General Alford seems especially upset that you called him out in that last post. Word to the wise, next time don't call out the man who is your convening authority."

"So, what happens next?"

"I think they are going to offer a special court-martial. I'll take a look at the offer and get back to you."

I went back to my cell and tried processing all the information that was thrown at me. It was overwhelming. I didn't have visitors over the weekend. I sat in my cell and thought out my next moves. Special court-martial was a misdemeanor. It was irrelevant. The only things that mattered were avoiding a guilty conclusion at general court-martial and receiving an honorable discharge. My retirement was gone regardless. What was my goal? Did I want to try and beat the Marine Corps, or was my message of accountability the most important thing? If I accepted a plea at special court-martial, they would let me out of jail immediately. I could show the generals what it looks like for an officer to accept accountability. Then I could lobby for an honorable discharge and go on with my life. If I fought the charges at general court-martial, I would remain in jail for another six months. If I was found guilty of just one of the multiple charges, it was a felony. The Marine Corps wouldn't allow me to have enlisted Marines in the jury. I could only have lieutenant colonels or higher-ranking officers. I already knew what that demographic thought of me. The special court-martial was the better play.

The next week I met with my lawyers. General Alford offered me a plea deal that involved five charges at special court-martial. I had to plead guilty to all of them and then sign a stipulation of facts. Then I would have to submit a resignation, and the characterization would later be determined between honorable and general under honorable.

"Give it to me. I'll sign it," I said.

"We can sit in here while you read it."

"Have you read it?"

"Yes."

"Does it matter if I disagree with any of the comments?"

"No. At this point, this is the deal. If we say no, we go to the general court-martial."

"Then give it to me. I'll sign it now."

I was out of jail on Tuesday, October 7. I spent a total of nine days in the jail. The first thing I did was drive to the house. I wanted to see Jackie and the kids. They hadn't been able to visit me while I was in jail. Jackie knew I was getting out of jail that day, but she decided to leave early to Virginia Beach with the kids without telling me. I called her while waiting at the house, "Jackie, are you at swim practice, cause I'm at the house waiting for you?"

"Oh sorry, babe. No, we didn't go to swim today. I took the kids up to Virginia Beach early. We didn't know what time you would get out, and I didn't want to make the kids wait around. So, we took off."

"OK," I said. "Call me when you get back in town."

I then drove back to the condo. My parents were there and eager to tell me about their media tour. I thanked them for all their efforts and then walked back to my bedroom. The next day Brian convinced me to bring on a team of lawyers that cumulatively charged me the price of an exotic car. I still have slight heartburn about the arrangement. But based on the generosity of the American people, it seemed like an easy decision. The new lawyers were very connected and engaged the media in creative ways that helped counter some of the narratives while I remained under the gag order. I worked with the whole team over Zoom every night. I met my new lawyers the day of my trial.

My court-martial was scheduled eight days after my release from jail. It was the fastest court-martial from plea agreement to court adjudication in the history of the Marine Corps. The Marine Corps wanted this saga to end, but they weren't done attacking me. Two days after I was released from jail, on October 9, *Task and Purpose* released another article about me. It was the same journalist, Jeff Schogol, who previously misreported about me. The new article was titled, "Leaked documents reveal just how concerned the Marine Corps was about Lt Col Stuart Scheller's call for revolution." The article stated, "They had received the investigation from a leaked source." Keep in mind, Jeff Schogol is the senior Pentagon reporter. This article came out exactly one week before my court-martial. The article stated that a senior officer had confirmed my support for the January 6 attacks and that I wanted to burn the system down with a well-trained group. The article then talks about the book *Imperium* in my third video and how it was written by a fascist. This connection to fascism allows the "journalist" to explicitly make a connection to Hitler.

My lawyers called *Task and Purpose* and asked them if they had my medical records since they stated they had my investigation. They refused to make a formal statement. Then on October 17, after the court-martial was complete, they updated the article. Instead of saying, "They received the investigation from a leaked source," they updated it to "They received legal documents from a leaked source." At the bottom of the article, they justified the correction based on previously reporting an incorrect number of charges against me. There is no mention of the correction between the modified terms "investigation" and "legal documents." This is relevant, because if they had the investigation, by proxy, they had received my medical records. They figured out late that this was illegal and that they had actually published the crime.

Days before the trial Colonel Hobbs also continued his attacks on my character. He told the *Washington Post*, "He hasn't shown one speck of remorse or admitted he was wrong in any way. I 100 percent believe it's a ploy for him to run for office." He went on to say, "I always told him how arrogant he was."

After reading it I thought, *You never said that. If you thought I was that arrogant, then why objectively and verifiably did you rate me as one of the best captains over your entire career? The last conversation we did have, you told me about how my racial pre-disposition led to ignorance. But I noticed you left that out.* I wasn't as mad as I was the first couple of times he attacked me. At this point it was a trend. I concluded the only rational way I could make sense of the situation; his racial hate allowed him to only see the things he wanted to see.

Monday, October 11, the week of my trial, Colonel Emmel finally emailed me a response to my request redress on why he had prevented me from bringing charges against General McKenzie. It stated, "You have suffered no wrong as defined by JAGINST 5800.7g. This command is under no legal obligation to assist you in preferring court-martial charges. You have no rights under these circumstances the violation of which could give rise to a claim of action by you." I always knew General Alford lacked the courage to take my charge sheet and refer charges against General McKenzie. But I wanted to make him publicly declare that he sought accountability against me and not General McKenzie. Illegally blocking my charge sheet prevented General Alford from addressing a tough public decision.

Later that night I stopped by my house. It was the last day my family was in town and only the second time I had seen them since being released from jail. The house had appraised, and the next family was moving in the following week. My wife was leaving by the end of the day to move to Virginia Beach for good. I came to spend the day with my children and gather that last few things out of my closet. My wife told me the kids had invited a bunch of friends over to the trampoline park as a going-away party. My second son was very upset because a girl he liked in his class didn't attend. My wife told me it was a general's daughter. "You don't realize that we are lepers here. Everyone knows about you. The kids were leaving the playground crying because all their class-mates were telling them that their dad was in jail. I need to get the kids out of town."

I walked into the other room, and my second son was crying, still upset that he was moving and the girl he liked didn't come see him off. Something about seeing him cry tore me apart. I started sobbing. I couldn't remain in the house. I ran to my truck and drove back to my condo. Later that night I gathered my emotions and went back to eat dinner with my family at Olive Garden. When we finished, I hugged all of them and said my goodbyes. My family took off that night. Later that night I texted Jackie and asked if she could come to the court-martial. I told her I understood at that point we were moving toward divorce, but I thought it would be helpful for her to hear my side of the story at the court-martial. She told me she couldn't. She had to get the kids on the bus for their new school. She asked if I would email my statement.

CHAPTER 17:

WHY DOES THE OATH MEAN SOMETHING DIFFERENT TO THEM?—COURT-MARTIAL. LETTER OF REPRIMAND. NARCISSISTIC.

"Moral Courage is the most valuable and usually the most absent characteristic in men."

—General Patton

The trial happened so quickly the prosecution couldn't provide the stipulation of facts (understanding between the prosecution and defense) until the morning of the trial. They did send me a version the day before trial, but it had verbiage about child pornography from someone else's charge sheet. They had copied and pasted from someone else's charge sheet and failed to take out the old verbiage. Despite how troubling that was for a couple of reasons, it didn't really matter. Once the charge sheet reflected my crimes and not those of some other individual, I signed without scruple the morning of the trial.

The trial was a circus. It was all for show. The outcome was predestined. The only real suspense was whether the judge agreed with the $30,000 fine requested by the prosecution. Media from all over the globe were staged at the entrance of the courtroom. Congressmen and -women all wanted to participate as witnesses. Many of their testimonies were more about them than they were about me. It also added to the narrative about my right-wing motives. I regretted allowing my lawyers convince me to use the members of Congress in my court-martial. The most important testimony came from the friends I called as witnesses. For example, Major Dave Borden who was injured in Iraq. Captain Matt Underhill who was a platoon commander with me in Iraq. Staff Sergeant Chris Ramsey who served with me Afghanistan. First Sergeant Dale Barbitta who was my senior enlisted in MARSOC. Those who actually knew me.

The commandant's lawyer showed up to support the prosecution. I'm not sure how frequently that happens, but it felt like the commandant wanted to ensure the prosecution had the best representation. The commandant's lawyer objected to everything. But again, the outcome was predestined. It was all for show.

Up to that point, I hadn't made any formal statements to the Marine Corps other than my social media posts. I refused to allow Colonel McCullar to interview me. I think the prosecution actually believed the narrative in the investigation. It was the prosecution's only reference point. When I started talking and offered counter perspectives, you could watch them scrambling. I told them about everything else my executive officer said the day I mentioned January 6. They asked for a recess as if they were going to call him in as a witness. I hoped they would. They didn't. This scenario kept playing out. They stated I wasn't returning Colonel Emmel's calls. This was verifiably false, and we said as much. I watched the prosecution call Colonel Emmel during the break, but again, they didn't want to bring him to the stand to rebut my statements. It was hard to illustrate all the lies and undue command influence while also pleading guilty. It was a fine line I actually tripped over a couple of times. But in the end, I think I made my point. I think they regretted allowing me a speaking platform.

I eventually delivered a ten-minute speech. I will directly quote the summation from that statement:

> This is not the America I know. This is not the America that I have fought so hard to defend the last seventeen years. In summary, I was never charged with a false official statement. Because everything I have said was true. If the Marine Corps could have charged me with false official statement, they would have. My statements all center around the fact that I did not believe General Officers were held to the same standards as junior leaders. I also believed, that similar to post Vietnam, the Marine Corps leadership was trying to spin the narrative about our failures on the junior officers and enlisted without taking a hard look at themselves. I also believed that once I spoke out, the Marine Corps wholistically took every opportunity to attack me, and never actually cared about my well being. But it's hard for the Marine Corps to defeat someone who refuses to quit. Going forward, I am still demanding accountability from my senior General officers. Since this endeavor began, not a single General officer has accepted accountability. Not a single General officer has contacted me directly in any forum to deescalate the situation. Since this endeavor began, I have acknowledged that I should be held accountable for my actions. I am standing here today pleading guilty. This is me accepting accountability. But it deeply pains me that my senior leaders are incapable of being as courageous. Without accountability from our senior leaders, the system cannot evolve, and the military will ultimately keep re-

peating the same mistakes in the future. It doesn't matter if a SSgt squad leader is highly efficient in distributed operations if the General officers have relegated themselves to "yes sir" responses. We need senior leaders who possess the moral courage to push back when something doesn't make sense. Furthermore, I understand that my process of criticism was unorthodox and not within official Marine Corps channels. I essentially requested mast in a very public setting. I acknowledge that it was potentially damaging to the Marine Corps' reputation. But I felt the conversation and need for change outweighed the potential negative bad press. I did what I did because I thought it was in the best long-term interest of the Marine Corps. I have always wanted to make the Marine Corps better. Not damage the Marine Corps. I acknowledge that my actions placed the Marine Corps in a position where they were forced to respond and couldn't quietly hide behind closed doors. My actions were very public, and at times, very emotional. But I think the emotional rollercoaster that I went through, is what every service member in the country goes through. The only difference is that my experience was very public. And unlike the twenty-two Service Members a day who kill themselves, I decided a long time ago that I will never be broken. No matter the struggle, I will prevail stronger. Post Traumatic Growth. But even with that mindset, that doesn't mean I don't experience pain. That doesn't mean I don't experience depression. That doesn't mean I don't take time to cry. If the leaders of the military actually cared about service members, and their sacrifices, all the current and previous senior leaders would engage in public discussions about the shortfalls in their decision making. Senior leaders accepting accountability would heal more service members than any other initiative. The junior service members deserve that from their leadership. I believed General officers demonstrated they are unable or unwilling to hold themselves accountable. As a result, I believed fundamental change needed to occur in the military. I am being held accountable for my actions. The General officers should be held accountable for their failures.

Despite this long speech, and many other statements I made over the two-day trial, it was clear some media showed up only to report their version of the story. The first day of the trial, I responded to a question saying, because "I was spinning out of control at that point." That comment was ripped out of context and used to describe me in over 50 percent of the articles. "Lieutenant Colonel Scheller, guilty of five charges, emotionally describes at trial how he was spinning out of control."

The judge, Colonel Hines, was a fair arbitrator. I was fortunate to have him look at all the facts of the case. It appeared to me that he didn't want me to plead guilty. He stated that, in his over thirty years as a JAG officer, he "had never seen someone sent to pre-trial confinement for these types of charges." He said General Alford listing himself as a victim on the charge sheet and maintaining his authority as the convening authority of the court-martial was bordering on illegal. He went on to say that after reviewing my record, it was one of the "most exemplary records he'd ever seen." He pointed out that the charge sheet took comments out of context. He also had something to say about the leaked investigation in the *Task and Purpose* article. He said the leaked documents were very disturbing. "It's unfair. It's illegal. And it needs to be investigated…it creates the specter of unlawful command influence." He ended up accepting my guilty pleas, but instead of fining me $30,000 as requested by the prosecution, he only fined me $5,000 and asked for the command to issue me a letter of reprimand.

I walked out of the court feeling victorious. When I got back to my condo that night, I texted every one of my friends who lied about me in the investigation. I had purposely waited to contact them until the court-martial was over so that the statements couldn't be used against me. All I needed to do was quote their lies back to them. None of them responded, but it made me feel better to let them know I knew they were fake.

The week following my court-martial, General Alford sent me my letter of reprimand. He stated:

> You have violated your solemn oath to support and defend the Constitution of the United States. Your actions have harmed good order and discipline within the service as well as publicly discredited the U.S. Marine Corps. Your narcissistic acts can serve only to erode the rule of law. You have failed in your duties to your command, fellow Marines, the U.S. Marine Corps, and the laws and traditions governing military service. For these reasons, you are hereby reprimanded.

It goes on to say:

> You may forward a statement concerning this letter for inclusion in your record within 15 days after receipt of this action…. In connection with your statement, any statement submitted shall be couched in temperate language and shall be confined to pertinent facts. Opinions shall not be expressed nor the motives of others impugned. Your statement shall not contain countercharges.

I responded:

> I object to the characterizations made. They
> do not accurately reflect my actions or my charac-
> ter. You characterized me as "narcissistic" which
> implies a psychological personality disorder. I
> am not narcissistic. I was not diagnosed with this
> condition after the mental health screening your
> command ordered me to undertake. Without of-
> fering my personal opinions on this matter, it is
> relevant to illustrate that you stated my response
> to your letter of reprimand "shall be couched
> in temperate language and shall be confined to
> pertinent facts." Yet in your letter of reprimand,
> you felt compelled to use the word "narcissistic"
> which is neither temperate nor confined to per-
> tinent facts.

Following the letter of reprimand, I finished my checkout items, and Colonel Emmel finally allowed me to take leave. The only pending item at that point was the characterization of discharge. The agreed-upon legal deal only allowed the Marine Corps a choice between honorable or general under honorable. The main difference was that general under honorable didn't allow me to enter the Reserves or National Guard in an attempt to circumvent the system and make it to my twenty-year retirement. I had the opportunity to write a letter to the secretary of the Navy outlining my case. The letter said the following:

> Sir:
>
> 1. I am submitting this letter formally request-
>   ing an honorable discharge in conjunction
>   with my resignation. I attempted to route
>   you a resignation package back in August

2021 for an exit date of September 11th, 2021, but due to my legal situation, this process took much longer than I anticipated. Yet despite my request for an honorable discharge, I can predict a different recommendation from my chain of command. Major General Alford will be the first recommending officer in my chain of command. However, it is my opinion that Major General Alford is not impartial in this matter. I base this opinion on his actions: Major General Alford relieved me of my command for a lack of trust and confidence within 18 hours of my first social media post. He did this without allowing any investigation to take place. Major General Alford also listed himself as a victim on the charge sheet of my court martial while still maintaining his position as the convening authority of the court martial. Additionally, Major General Alford was the officer in charge of my command investigation. He then either actively or negligently allowed that command investigation, which by his direction included my medical records, to be leaked to the media. While a separate investigation on the leaked command investigation has been initiated, the results of that separate investigation will not be attached to this resignation package. Additionally, Major General Alford called me a narcissist in his issued letter of reprimand and refused to acknowledge my request to allow an impartial officer to write my letter of reprimand. It is very clear that

Major General Alford will recommend a general discharge with honorable conditions, which is the lowest characterization he is allowed to recommend in our agreed upon legal deal. I also feel that once he makes that recommendation, the remainder of the General Officers in the chain of command will lack the moral courage to disagree with the recommendation of the first General Officer in the chain of command. As such, I predict the recommendation from the General Officers of the Marine Corps concerning my characterization of discharge will be a general discharge under honorable conditions.

    a.   Despite the ease and speed at which Major General Alford held me accountable, he then refused to allow me to prefer charges against General McKenzie even though it is my legal right to do so according to rule 307(a) of the Manual for Courts Martial. Refer to refence (b) for the command's formal response to my request. The command's deliberate avoidance of the issue is surprising based on their zest for accountability. I felt, and still feel, that it's important to hold General McKenzie accountable. General McKenzie publicly acknowledged his evacuation plan required the Taliban for perimeter security, and that this plan ultimately, and quite foreseeably, contributed to the deaths of thirteen service members. After failing to implement a tactically effective security plan, he then publicly stated that he left behind hundreds of American citizens and billions of dollars of equipment in Afghanistan because he believed the Department of State was a viable option to complete the military objectives of the withdraw. Yet, the Secretary of State in Congressional testimony weeks later admitted that he did not inherit a plan, nor was he fully prepared to evacuate the remainder of Americans and allies left in Afghanistan. And as if that wasn't enough, General McKenzie was then forced to acknowledge that he was responsible for only killing civilians and children with a drone strike executed in response to the avoidable attack at the airfield. He publicly stated, "it was a mistake and I offer my sincerest apology." If the aforementioned list of failures isn't enough for a General Officer to be held accountable, what could it possibly take? Service members all understand mistakes happen in war, but they deserve more than hollow apologies and hand waves. Service members' mental health requires moral courage and accountability from senior leaders. I acknowledge that General McKenzie was restrained by the resources imposed by the President in the withdraw, but that cannot excuse the execution. When General McKenzie was presented with the resources and restraints of the situation, he had the option to resign, or to accept the consequences of his plan. While General McKenzie serves at the pleasure of the President, nothing is stopping the military from preferring charges, or for General McKenzie to hold himself accountable. General McKenzie could hold himself accountable and still maintain his retirement unlike me. General McKenzie could hold himself accountable and not have to argue for an honorable discharge unlike me. This double standard of accountability must be acknowledged, or our military is destined for failure and the suicide rates in the veteran community will continue to rise.

2. I do not feel the General Officers in my chain of command are impartial nor will they remain objective. As such, I feel it relevant to offer the opinions and statements of

Colonel Hines, the Military Judge who presided over my Court Martial, quoted from reference (a).

a. The Military Judge noted concerning the leaked command investigation and medical records, "I don't know if that's true or not...but the truth is these statements went unrebutted from the government. I don't know what the government's response to that would be. But that fact is that's very disturbing. It's unfair. It's illegal. And it needs to be investigated.... It creates the specter of unlawful command influence."

b. The Military Judge noted that by Major General Alford acting as the Convening Authority in a case where he also considered himself a victim gave a strong appearance of a conflict of interest.

c. The Military Judge noted concerning the videos..."those videos are a lot longer, and are more extensive, and place into more appropriate context the specific statements that were charged and criminalized in this case."

d. The Military Judge noted concerning my service, "I went through [Lt-

Col Scheller's] record last night...I read his fitness reports. What it appears to the court is that this is a seventeen-year Marine who had an outstanding record before this one-month course of conduct. I don't think I've ever seen anyone consistently marked in the top three marks of the Christmas Tree in the Reviewing Officer Evaluations. Glowing comments from Reporting Seniors and Reviewing Officers consistently. A career that appeared to the court to be on the upward slope until the last month."

3. I am a command selected battalion commander. This recent battalion command selection implies, according to my previous service record, and according to the opinions of the distinguished senior officers serving on the Marine Corps command board, that I am in the top 20% of my peer group. I was screened and selected for resident military education at each opportunity. At Command and Staff college, I received a master's in military science. My thesis paper focused on how to make the Department of Defense and American foreign policy more effective. I served as a company commander for a cumulative of five years. During one of those company command tours, I was recommended and submitted for the Left-

wich Award, as noted in my fitness reports, because the command felt I was the best company commander in the Marine Corps. I served in MARSOC as a senior leader preparing small teams to deploy around the globe. I was hand selected to serve as a Regimental Operations Officer. Furthermore, I deployed five times. In that time, I spent more than a year and a half living on Naval Ships. In that time, I also spent a cumulative of 19 months living in Iraq and Afghanistan. Furthermore, I have evacuated American citizens in harm's way during non-combatant evacuations. I have conducted hurricane relief during humanitarian operations. I have conducted bilateral training operations with foreign nations across the globe. I have a bronze star. I have an Army Commendation with Valor. I have three Meritorious Service Medals. I have three Navy Commendations. I have lived in conditions that required me to eat only MREs, breath burning feces, and bath with only baby wipes for months. I have personally killed the Nation's enemies with a rifle in the dirt. I have been part of groups that have killed the Nation's enemies with indirect fire, with SUAS, and with Machine Gun fire. I have personally stepped on IEDs that did not detonate. I have watched service members die in front of me. I have carried allied troops in body bags for miles when helicopter evacuations were not available to pick up our dead during dismounted patrols. I was once forced to sleep in a body bag spooning another man after being left on a mountain with inadequate supplies to prevent from freezing. I was on a combat patrol in Afghanistan while missing the birth of my first child. I have sat with close friends in Walter Reed after suicide vest attacks. I have had close friends killed. I am part of generation who participated in our wars on the ground, instead of from safe distances in Combat Operation Centers like many of our current senior leaders. And yet, despite all my sacrifices and service to this Nation, or perhaps because of it, I feel that discussing the lack of accountability following the failed Afghanistan withdraw is more important than my personal retirement or stability. Ultimately, I feel there will always be another imminent enemy facing the United States. And to be clear, I fully believe that a strong military arm of foreign diplomacy is critical for the strength of a free democratic nation. But I offer a dangerous caveat to this belief: if our military leaders consistently distract the Nation by perceived threats of the future while simultaneously failing to hold senior leaders accountable for the mistakes of our past wars, our Nation is destined to repeat the same mistakes going forward.

4. I also want to state formally that I am not a victim. I made choices understanding full well the implication of my actions. I stated my understanding of the consequences in my

first video. However, I still publicly posted the message despite the potential impact on my personal and professional life, and the potential impact on good order and discipline within the military. I weighed this cost against the potential gains our military could achieve from addressing and developing shortfalls in the current leadership. There are critical times in our Republic when military officers should carefully examine their sworn oath to the Constitution against all enemies foreign and domestic. It's been very painful to witness the obedience and fear within my generation of officers despite our sacrifices in the Global War on Terrorism. Furthermore, I have never been charged with a false official statement. While I have taken accountability for my actions, I want to be clear, I am not remorseful for publicly speaking hard truths. I feel very strongly that someone in our military organization needed to illustrate the current leadership failures. While it may not have been my place to say what needed to be said...there was no one else in a current position of authority with the courage to say it. As such, I believe it is easier for current military leaders to condemn my actions, because to agree with it would force a recognition of their own shortcomings.

5. I believe by the regulations governing our Department of Navy, I deserve an honorable discharge. However, I understand the influ-

ence you are probably receiving on this matter from the President of the United States, who to be clear, I have never publicly attacked, despite being the first officer in the military charged with Article 88 since the Vietnam War. I have too much respect for civilian authority over the military and the office of the President to point out perceived mistakes from the same individual who recommended you to your position. I also understand the influence you are probably receiving on this matter from the Secretary of Defense, who I have repeatedly pointed out has a conflict of interest with his previous position as the former Raytheon Board Director. It is not lost on me that the Secretary of Defense is the leader who swore you into office. I also understand the pressure you are probably receiving from the General Officers in the Marine Corps; General Officers whose mistakes and hypocritical leadership styles I have consistently illustrated. Furthermore, I understand the perception some might develop when looking at your long list of donations and support to the Democratic Party. I further understand the perception some might develop when looking at the long list of government contracts developed with the Department of Defense through SBG Technology. But despite all the potential influences on this matter, I want to believe the military is not political or beholden to big industry. I believe your military background and loyalty to the Navy will guide your impartial conclusions on this matter. I believe you will only use the orders governing our Department of Navy to guide your decision. And finally, I want to state for the record how deeply moved I am by your life accomplishments since you migrated to the United States from Cuba. Truly. Your humble beginnings, service to our country, and subsequent accomplishments as an entrepreneur should be an inspiration to ALL Americans. Your story epitomizes why the American dream is still worth fighting for.

6. I am respectfully asking that you reference SECNAV Instruction regulation 1920.6D enclosure (8) subsection (c) which authorizes you to categorize my service as honorable if, "the officer's record is otherwise so meritorious that under the particular circumstances any other characterization would be clearly inappropriate." My record of service leading up to 26 August 2021 speaks for itself. No other clarifications are required.

7. I remain truly humbled and appreciative of the opportunity to have commanded Marines within the Department of the Navy. I remain Semper Fidelis.

I routed the letter through Colonel Emmel to General Alford. Then I waited. During this time, my parents with their new celebrity started a movement to call the secretary of the Navy's office demanding "an honorable discharge and quick release of LtCol Scheller." The secretary of the Navy's office received hundreds of calls a day. The office eventually replaced the sailors with Marines to answer the phones.

As I waited for the discharge, the Marine Corps completed another "investigation" on how my first investigation and medical records ended up with *Task and Purpose*. The man who did the investigation was LtCol Matthew "Bubba" Cook. Despite how the leak negatively and prejudicially impacted me, LtCol Cook stated that he could find no evidence of the leak from the Marine Corps, and thus concluded that it was most likely leaked from my defense counsel. The Commanding General, who replaced General Alford at Marine Corps Installations East, very quickly agreed, and decided no further investigation was necessary on the matter. Cowards.

It is also relevant to note that when the resignation package routed to Headquarters Marine Corps, it was missing certain paperwork. One of the legal assistants at Headquarters Marine Corps had a special relationship with my lawyer. When she realized the package was inconsistent, she called him to discuss the matter. In that conversation, my lawyer realized my letter to the secretary of the Navy and my response to the letter of reprimand were not routed in the resignation package. *How could they do that?* I wondered. *This is dealing with my entire life.* Still under a gag order, and deciding to work within the system this time, I submitted a request mast form to speak with the commandant. Request mast is a formal process in the Marine Corps that allows Marines an audience with the generals for a complaint. Many people after my first video said I should have worked within the system, which would have been the request mast process. The order states that you can request an audience with leadership up to the level where a reasonable resolution will be adjudicated. The order also states that the first general officer can deny the request. But I knew General Alford and General Kevin Iiams had not routed the correspondence, so I felt like the only person who could adjudicate my complaint was the commandant.

Colonel Emmel called me into his office to discuss the adjudication of my request mast. My request mast was denied by General Alford because "commanders may deny a request mast that has at its core a grievance involving involuntary administrative discharge proceedings, whether contemplated, pending, in progress, or final."

"Sir, I don't understand on so many levels. One, my complaint dealt with General Alford, so why can't I go above him? Two, if my complaint has to do with my discharge, which by the way affects my whole life, then how do I address the issue? Third, I'm not being involuntarily separated. I agreed to resign. There is a difference. And four, why didn't he at least get on a video conference to discuss this with me face-to-face? Is he scared of me?"

"Stu, you have no recourse here. Do you have any other questions?"

I walked out of the office. That was the last time I ever saw Colonel Emmel face-to-face.

As I predicted in my letter to the secretary of the Navy, General Alford, General Iiams, and the commandant, General Berger, all requested a general under honorable discharge. But as it went up to the secretary of the Navy's office, Carlos Del Toro refused to engage with the document. He had an assistant endorse the recommendation of the generals from the Marine Corps. Coward.

December 23, 2021, I was discharged from the Marines. As I departed, I made the following post still hanging on my social media:

> It was December 23rd, of 1776. The Americans were fighting for liberty and freedom against an old hypocritical government. Up to that point in the struggle, the Americans suffered a series of defeats. But George Washington, undeterred, mobilized his force for a surprise attack over the holidays. The attack on December 26th wasn't decisive, but as history shows, it was a turning point in the war.

To recap my series of defeats after demanding accountability; I was relieved of command, slandered as homicidal/suicidal by the USMC's public affairs team, ordered to get a mental health evaluation, lied about in the investigation by my "friends", denied my legal right to prefer charges against another service member beholden to the UCMJ, imprisoned under the false pretense of "flight risk", left without basic items in prison for five days, offered a legal deal while held illegally in jail (you can't be placed in pre-trial for a special court martial), slandered again when my medical records and investigation were released to the media, fined 5K dollars, called a narcissist in my letter of reprimand, kept under a gag order for over four months, denied the ability to request mast twice, given the lowest characterization (General under Honorable Conditions) allowed by the plea deal, and lost my retirement. Was it worth it? Well...unfortunately for them...the war isn't over. I think we just arrived at a turning point. The old system underestimated US then...and they underestimate US now.

I was released from the Marine Corps today, Thursday, December 23rd, 2021. I am filled with mixed emotions. I would like to sincerely thank the Marine Corps for forging me into a man. And from the bottom of my heart, I'd like to thank all the Marines who served, led, bled, and suffered alongside me the past 17 years.

I'd also like to thank the 40K Americans who donated to my foundation while I was in jail. Witnessing Americans of all ethnicities, political parties, and backgrounds donate to my fund, fills my heart with love for Americans. Your support not only paid for my lawyers but will provide stability for my family as I move on to the next chapter in my life. I hope to meet every person who donated and thank them. I promise to spend the rest of my life delivering a return on that investment. I'd also like to thank the thousands of people who called their congressional representative or military leadership on my behalf. Your support was instrumental in enabling my release from the institution.

Out of respect to my senior leaders, I haven't done a single interview since this began. But now it's my turn. My television media blitz starts with Tucker Carlson on 4 January. Leading up to my TV interviews, I plan to make a post a day up to the date of my interviews starting with the 26th, the day of George Washington's attack. 2022 is the start of a new year. It's the start of a new generation. The lions are home from war. And we aren't assimilating anymore.

We Can't All Be Wrong. O-O. Mid-game starts now.

COUNTERARGUMENTS

"Ordinary men, who normally follow the imitative of others, tend to lose self-confidence when they reach the scene of action: things are not what they expected, the more so as they still let others influence them. But even the man who planned the operation and now sees it being carried out may well lose confidence in his earlier judgment. War has a way of masking the stage with scenery crudely daubed with fearsome apparitions. Once this is cleared away, and the horizon becomes unobstructed, developments will confirm his earlier convictions."

—Carl von Clausewitz in *On War*

There are a few common counterarguments I'd like to address. The first argument centers around the utility of such an endeavor. Many people who agreed with the content of my statements also believed challenging the system was not worth the sacrifice. My "friend" Lieutenant Colonel Jeff Cummings texted this sentiment as I went through the ordeal. Based on his eagerness to talk about my situation with the investigating officer, his statement can be found in the investigation: "There's just going to be one less LtCol. I don't really see the point."

I fundamentally and philosophically disagree with the logic. I acknowledge there are times the following clichés apply: "pick your battles" and "you can be right and still be wrong." But ultimately, we as Americans must apply judgment and realize there are other exceptional times when people must make a choice between personal values and the values espoused by the bureaucracy no matter the cost. For all the talk of moral courage and ethics during annual training, somehow the military demonstrated public perception was more important than moral courage.

An extension of this argument is built around the principle that our military and political systems are "just the way they are, and you can't change them." If Americans relegate themselves to this defeatist mentality, America truly is lost. Relying on senior leaders to change systems that inherently protects senior leaders' power is misguided. I swear to support and defend the Constitution, against all enemies, foreign and domestic. I believe the power of the government comes from the people. However, both principles are hinged upon the belief that people will speak up when grave injustice threatens the evolution of our representative democracy. Reflecting back, I shouldn't have used the word "revolution" at the end of some posts. My use of that word was always about bringing fundamental change to the system. A better word is "evolution."

Second, many people argued they agreed with the content of my statements but disagreed with the delivery. They argued I should have written an article in a formal military publication or used one of the formal processes in the military to address my complaints. I believe these critics lack perspective. Fundamental change has never occurred in the military from professional articles. Fundamental change occurs through action. Through courage. Furthermore, I hope my story about the investigation, request redress, and request mast processes illustrates how fundamentally flawed the formal complaint processes are in the military. If you point out the shortfalls of senior leaders, the formal complaint processes won't help you.

Third, many people brought up that it wasn't my place to make such a statement. That statements of foreign policy are reserved for general officers and politicians. "Mid-grade officers shouldn't be offering opinions on foreign policy." My response to those people is simple, "Which one of those senior officers spoke up? And if none of them did, perhaps we need mid-grade officers with moral courage." Do senior officers possess such deep understanding of oaths, strategy, justice, and morality that the rest of the military force should remain silent?

I last spoke face-to-face with General Alford in the bar at The Basic School. He had ideas for training infantry that were "revolutionary" from the antiquated-system perspective. But understanding the bureaucratic game, he issued the intent, "We can't move too fast. We can't scare the children." I wrote down the guidance. I thought about the guidance. I concluded that the guidance perfectly epitomized the systemic restraints on progress. My counterargument to that guidance is the following: "If the children's lives are in danger, and scaring them forces a change in behavior that saves their lives down the road... I hope we all are courageous enough to scare the children despite judgment from the scared and uninformed."

Another argument often levied against me was, "Why now? You have served in failed wars your entire career, and you just now chose to speak up. Why?" This argument allowed many people to conclude my motives were political. But again, I fundamentally disagree with the logic. We should hope our senior leaders develop a deeper appreciation for the situation and speak out against previous mistakes, especially if they participated in the mistakes. There were multiple off ramps in Afghanistan that could have allowed America to declare success. Task Force 58, commanded by General Mattis, could have won the war in the opening gambit. But we failed. Then again, we had an opportunity to off ramp after killing Osama bin Laden. General Mattis served as the CENTCOM combatant commander during the Osama bin Laden raid. Had he said, "I have led these wars for the last eight years, and I was wrong. Our counterinsurgency tactics cannot reasonably be linked to the strategical political objectives, and thus I recommend we end these wars now," I would have celebrated him as a hero. That would have demonstrated moral courage. That would have demonstrated the foresight academics try to credit him with. But then again, that probably wouldn't have led to a board member position at General Dynamics.

Furthermore, many people said they agreed with the content of the first video, but they didn't understand any of my actions following the first video. They felt I was reckless, and it took away from the valid content of my first video. I struggle with this argument the most. My response to these critics would be, when you're in a near ambush, you assault through the objective. You run more risk trying to retreat. Allowing myself to silently submit after being fired and ridiculed by former mentors was an attack on my initial statement. It was an attack on me personally. There is nothing more personal to me than my honor and service to this country. There is nothing more important to me than leaving this country in better shape for my sons than what I inherited from my father. My grandfather shaped my American way of life on the beaches of Normandy. Evolution only happens through struggle. I am willing to fight to the end for the things I believe in. I have never apologized, and I never will. I took accountability for my actions. I would have changed the way I delivered verbiage at certain points, but I don't regret what happened. Posttraumatic growth. I will only come out of this stronger. My hope is that America, Americans, and the American military will come out of this stronger.

Finally, many people believe I abandoned my family. This argument hurts the most. I love my family more than anything. People said to me, "You seem to care more about the thirteen service members who got killed than you do your own family." Reflecting back, it's true I made decisions that didn't include my wife. I made those decision based on a deep understanding of how she would react had I spoken to her. But I decided to speak out anyway, in part anticipating her anger but hoping that we would be able to reconcile. At this point, that doesn't seem likely. That being said, she was put in a terrible position by my actions but also by the military as well. The sacrifices she made over my seventeen-year career were immense. She will always be the mother of my children. She is truly a good person, despite a very challenging ordeal. Not included in the story are all the death threats, phone calls from my "friends" pointing out how I was suffering a mental breakdown, and media heckling her through this whole process. She went through a lot.

To the critics who say I abandoned my family, I'm not sure I agree. I hope one day my sons realize I attempted something morally courageous and that I did it to leave them a better future. My life and actions inherently become a road map for their future. My legacy as a father is defined by my actions, not by my quiet beliefs. I hope my sons take that lesson forward in life. The masses providing commentary on the sidelines are irrelevant. The world is defined by the brave people willing to act. I don't think I abandoned my family. I think I fought for my family. I always have, and always will, love my family.

THE WAY FORWARD

"Do not believe anything merely because you are told it is so, because others believe it, because it comes from tradition, or because you have imagined it. Do not believe what your teacher tells you merely out of respect. Believe, take for your doctrine, and hold true to that, which, after serious investigation, seems to you to further the welfare of all beings."

—Jean-Yves Leloup, *Compassion and Meditation*

Moving forward, I will continually advocate for change within the military system. America's foreign diplomacy model requires effective utilization of the military source of national power. The model created post World War II has consistently demonstrated failure. Senior military leaders and civilian-appointed officials at the highest levels of our key bureaucracies are so deep in their understanding of the system's intricacies, they have blinded themselves to the obvious shortfalls of the current system. The issues must be a grave concern for all Americans. We cannot allow senior military leaders to continually deflect blame for failed wars. Yes, there are fundamental problems with the entire "whole of government" foreign policy approach. Yes, civilian leadership ultimately makes the decisions. But no, this cannot continually be used as excuse for senior military leaders' failure.

I illustrated fundamental reforms required in the military culture and general-officer ranks. I used my personal story as mechanism to pull out key trends in the military establishment. The current senior leaders within the military establishment will not implement required change at the pace our nation demands. The military will only reform when the American people demand reform from their congressional representatives. The American people must tell their representatives to use the defense budget as the lever to implement changes. The military needs dramatic changes in the following thirteen areas:

1. Warfighting focus should be clarified as the priority. All other distractions should be minimized.

2. Overhaul the promotion system in all military services. A boss's assessment may be a factor in promotion, but so should warfighting performance. Develop warfighting games pitting leaders against each other. Make it truly free play. The winner must demonstrate performance though action, not assessment through the eyes of a boss. Winner receives preferential treatment in promotion. Furthermore, if there continues to be board selection for command and/or promotion chaired by other senior military officers, make it completely transparent how these senior military officers vote. Force them to demonstrate moral courage. Allowing senior leaders to hide behind a secret vote degrades the very transparency our system needs.

3. Promote based on performance, not time based. Implement this immediately. Any military member should be able to 'try out' for higher ranks during the wargame competition. Move talented leaders up more quickly. This will do more for retaining talent than all other initiatives. This will also marginalize the problem of nepotism. This will also marginalize the weight given to specific career paths.

4. Overhaul the screening process for officers at Officer Candidate School. Drill instructors are not the people we need screening officers' potential ability. Send all Marines to the same boot camp. Following boot camp, those who want to try out for the officer-screening portion should be given the opportunity. A college degree should not be a requirement. If the college degree is as valuable as we think, it should translate to better performance during the officer screening.

5. Establish a baseline threshold for tactical failure that results in the relief of a general officer and develop a separate process for it to occur. The president should always retain the right to fire a general. But the commander in chief is very unlikely to fire a general for a war's failure if this reflects on his own failure. So, what other governmental agency is holding them accountable? If the list from the Afghanistan evacuation isn't enough, what does it take to fire a general?

6. Throw out "just war theory." Replace it with "just win war theory."

7. Review the military education system. Remove the preponderance of civilian PhDs without military experience. Challenge students on an individual level. Allow the students to move at the pace of their ability, not the pace of the group. Revamp the operational planning qualification. Figure out a way to hold "operational planners" responsible for failed plans. Saying, "We offered multiple plans, so it's not our fault," is also not good enough. The team wins and loses together.

8. Dismantle and rebuild the procurement, purchasing, and budgeting process in the military. Give each commander a budget, and don't remove and/or reallocate funds at the end of a fiscal year. Reward efficient spending. Reward more competition within the oligopoly of firms competing for contracts. Allow more freedom for open purchases.

9. Update the military justice system or provide lawyers and investigators not dependent upon the system for promotion. Initiatives taking sexual assault out of military commander's hands only addresses a symptom of the broken system. Start by updating how command investigations are conducted. Command investigations no longer provide justice. They paint only what the commander wants to see. Reexamine internal processes for complaints by the junior service member and how they are addressed. Furthermore, start prosecuting commanders who illegally influence the outcome of the trial before due process.

10. Prevent general officers from taking board member positions as soon as they retire. If we can't prevent it, take their retirement. They can choose what's more important.

11. Develop combat standards that all genders and ethnicities must achieve. Separate standards for genders and ethnicities degrade the very principle of a warfighting focus.

12. Identify toxic leaders in the O-6 and above ranks. Fire them immediately. Replace them with talented field-grade officers. Then cancel the annual training on bullying. The problem will solve itself with better senior leadership.

13. Legislate a new system of foreign diplomacy. Goldwater-Nichols is not sufficient. America loses wars between the political and military seams. A whole-of-government approach needs to be developed now more than ever.

To the next president of the United States. If the generals convince you their model is better, I offer this challenge. Allow me to recruit and train a unit. The best people will make my team. It won't be hard to find recruits for my team. I have a long list of superior warfighters sitting in the fringes, forced out of the current military system due to a lack of conformity. Allow me a sliver of a normal comparative budget. Allow me to challenge at random a normal infantry unit at the appropriate phase of their deployment cycle within each service. I will pick a "qualified" unit as reported on by the defense report cards. I'll challenge your pick for secretary of defense in the very competition I'm advocating for. I'll demonstrate with performance that my ideas are better.

Chess Moves:

E4 Displayed in second video August 28th

Bg5 Displayed in second video August 28th

Bxf6 End of mental health post August 30th

C4 End of post to General Berger August 31st (later deleted)

Nf3 End of remain committed to accountability post September 2nd

E3 End of Labor Day post September 5th

Bxc4 Text of fourth video post September 16th

Displayed entire chess board in picture attached to post baiting command to send me to jail September 25th (later deleted)

Be2 Placed in SSIC of heading in letter to Secretary of Navy November 19th

O-O End of exiting Marine Corps post December 23rd. Stated "Mid-game starts now."

Nbe2... End of this book

ENDNOTES

1   General James L. Jones Jr., "All Elements of National Power: Moving To-ward a New Interagency Balance for US Global Engagement," Atlantic Council Combatant Command Task Force, Brent Scowcroft Center on International Security, July 22, 2014, https://www.atlanticcouncil.org/wp-content/uploads/2014/07/All_Elements_of_National_Power.pdf.

2   Michael E. Porter, "The Competitive Advantage of Nations," *Harvard Business Review* (March–April 1990), https://hbr.org/1990/03/the-competitive-advantage-of-nations.

3   Gabriel Marcella, "Understanding the Interagency Process: The Challenge of Adaptation," in *Affairs of State: The Interagency and National Security,* ed. Gabriel Marcella (Carlisle, Pennsylvania: Strategic Studies Institute, 2008), 17.